Judy

Best wishes

Caroline

Aug/08

SHADOWS IN EVERY CORNER

By

CATHERINE ASHFORD

authorHOUSE

1663 Liberty Drive, Suite 200
Bloomington, Indiana 47403
(800) 839-8640
www.authorhouse.com

First published by AuthorHouse 08/06/04

ISBN: 1-4184-7846-6 (sc)

Printed in the United States of America
Bloomington, Indiana

This book is printed on acid-free paper.

To protect my family, names have been changed.

About the Book

This is the true story of a young girl brought up in the strict and harsh life of a Catholic orphanage in the aftermath of the First World War, and of her struggle for survival.

Told by the nuns she was an orphan, she set out to search for her roots realizing that an overwhelming desire within her forced her onward, if only to prove them wrong.

Her perilous journeys through war-torn London, and monumental struggle against the Catholic authorities in her search for kith and kin, lasted over forty years. But for the kindness of Mr.Angus Baxter, a Genealogist living in Lakefield, Ontario, those tightly-held doors that were now opened, may have been closed forever.

As the years rolled by her search for family became a way of life, even after emigrating to Canada in 1967. Her indomitable spirit urged her to make the pilgrimage back to the land of her birth, every other year, with little success.

Eventually reaching her early sixties, and in possession of valuable information through Mr.Baxter who was unable to help her further, she hired the services of a Mr.Wilks, a researcher, living in Kent. In 1990, she received news from him that her parents, whom she had spent a lifetime searching for, had passed on. Further details from Mr.Wilks was to send shock waves through her, leaving her speechless in disbelief. While searching the records he found the birth certificate of a brother, who was unknown to her. Born in 1919, he would be seventy-two years of age at the time. Was it possible that by some miracle, he was still alive?

The Search Begins

By the time I reached sixteen years of age, I had spent all but two years of my young life in the somewhat questionable care of nuns at an orphanage in a small village in the County of Kent, England. From there, I was sent 'out into the world' of which I knew little or nothing about, and had not even been prepared for. Having no choice whatsoever, I was put into domestic service where I remained in that position for eighteen months. Many years later, I would be shocked to hear my first place of employment was that of a reformatory school for unruly boys.

Owing to an order from the British Parliament that all young people over the age of sixteen must report to the nearest Labour Exchange for essential war work, I managed to extricate myself as quickly as possible from domestic service. Giving me a train voucher, an office clerk at the Labour Exchange told me to report for work at an aircraft factory in Weybridge, Surrey, where I would be forced to stay until hostilities ended.

In July 1944, a few months after my marriage, I was seized by a compulsive urge to trace the whereabouts of my parents whom I understood had lived in London. During this period the Second World War now in its fifth year, battled on in Europe, causing chaos with the lives of all people.Rationing in Britain made life intolerable for everyone, and although most of the people were willing to help their country in every possible way, the toughest part of surviving, for many, was to stay alive and keep oneself warm. This wasn't easy, as coal or any other form of heating was in short supply and this caused many hardships during the very cold winters of the 1940s. I remember wearing a pair of men's old, thick socks in bed and knitted woollen gloves with the fingers cut off, that had seen better days, which I had found by sheer luck; a luxury I silently guarded.

Regardless of whatever hurdles I had to cross in the search for my parents, it didn't dawn on me at that time the risks I would have to take. The train that travelled from Surrey to London, on the Aldershot, Hampshire line, was always jammed-packed with soldiers, and became an on-going target during the bombings. A main concern was to get to London as quickly as possible and, hopefully, in one piece. However, if a bomb landed near any of the railway lines during the journey, the train would come to a shrieking halt, scattering passengers everywhere.

Once over the shock, heads would peer out of the train windows to see at which station the train had stopped. What surprised most travellers, though, was how quickly the railway lines were cleared of debris when a bomb fell, and how little behind schedule the train was, when reaching its destination. Although I travelled the line from Surrey to Waterloo, many times, I was always horrified to see en route the destruction of homes, indeed entire streets, caused by these bombings.

It was during one such trip, that armed with the only information I possessed – a piece of paper showing the place of my baptism – I began the search for my parents. I knew that I had been baptized in the Roman Catholic Church of The English Martyrs at Walworth in the East End of London, but wasn't quite sure how to get there from Waterloo station. After making several inquiries to passersby, I was told to catch a certain bus that would put me down within a five minute walk to the church. When arriving at the church I noticed the priests' house was closeby, so I went up to the front door and knocked on it. As the door slowly opened, a young priest was standing inside. Asking if there was anything he could do for me, I explained to him briefly the reason for my unannounced visit and questioned if it was possible to have the parish records checked in order to confirm the accuracy of my baptism. Inviting me into a small library, the priest took down from a bookshelf a large black binder covering religious ceremonies that were held in the mid-1920s, and studied it carefully. After checking the records for a few minutes, he told me he couldn't find any entry of my parents as having been parishioners at his church. Neither could he enlighten me as to my parents' identity or whereabouts. Thanking the priest for his help, and leaving a small donation, I left the presbytery feeling this was not a good beginning and that, perhaps, I had wasted my journey.

Mulling over my thoughts while homeward-bound to Surrey I decided the next course of action would be to obtain a copy of my birth certificate at the earliest opportunity so I travelled to Somerset House in London, where all births, marriages and deaths records are kept. Upon arriving, I went straight to one of the 'enquiry' windows and asked the clerk how I would go about obtaining a birth certificate. Handing me an official application form, she told me to fill in all my details. I could only enter my name, date of birth and give scant information. Duly completed, and together with the required fee, I handed the form back to the clerk and was advised the certificate would be forwarded by mail, within two or three weeks.

Waiting impatiently for the document, the day finally arrived mid-week when an official-looking brown envelope was pushed through the letterbox of my front door. Excited, I picked it up off the mat, ran upstairs to the quiet of my bedroom, closed the door, and sat down on the double bed. With shaking fingers I tore open the envelope, fearful of what secrets it held, and glued my eyes to the document.

Scrutinizing and absorbing every detail, I learned my parents full names and where they had lived at the time of my birth. I also learned my true name was Catherine and not Carrie, which everyone at the orphanage had called me throughout my childhood. One thing firmly established, I was a Londoner. Carefully folding the document and returning it inside the envelope, I slid it for safe-keeping, beneath some lingerie in one of my dressing table drawers. With the information I now obtained of where my parents lived in 1925, the thought of finding them and actually seeing them excited me. It seemed worth searching this area first.

The following Monday, with no rain clouds in sight, I arose early in order to have sufficient time to dress, leisurely. Determined to create a good impression on my parents, I put on my one and only two-piece suit, which I reserved for special occasions. It was patterned in small checks, in colours of grey and mauve. Using sparse make-up, and taking a last look at the mirror, I assured myself that my appearance would meet with their approval.

Mimicking a businessman's attire, I took from the wardrobe a rolled-up umbrella, also grey, which blended well with my outfit and gave me, I thought, an air of distinction. Using my umbrella as a walking stick, I wended my way to Walton station and mingled with the early morning business crowd, on the platform. Looking well-groomed and feeling somewhat smug, there were no doubts in my mind that I would, and always would, rise to the occasion like anyone else, when needed.

Boarding the Waterloo train, I took a seat close to the window. As I sat watching the landscape flashing by, endless questions raced through my head at a speed which equalled that of the train as it charged from one station to the next. I wondered what my parents looked like, and how they would react when told I was their daughter. Would they accept me or simply deny all knowledge of my existence, thereby closing the door? Perhaps an embarrassment of their painful past, now anxious to catch up with them, would indicate a wish to disown me. Nevertheless, to all these questions, it was a chance I was prepared to take, whatever the consequence.

I was impatient for the train to arrive, yet at the same time I experienced a feeling of unease about my first visit to parents whom I had never known. Perhaps I should have written, beforehand, a letter of my intended visit, rather than appearing out of the blue on their front doorstep. As the train crawled into the station, I was compelled to go on.

Leaving the station and noting the Parliament Buildings on the right, I turned left and walked under a railway bridge. This led me into Westminster Bridge Road, the address shown on my birth certificate. I began checking the house numbers, my heart thumping, looking for No.72. Walking less than five minutes, the houses suddenly seemed to disappear; No.72 was nowhere in sight. Looking around, I wondered what to do next as all I could see on the ground was a large, solid block of concrete. Staring hard at it for a second or two I surmised I had turned, unknowingly, from Westminster Bridge Road into another road, and was about to walk away from the block when a worker, wearing a grubby cloth cap, walked towards me. I asked him if he knew where No.72 house was, and told him I was trying to find my parents. Giving me a strange look, and without hesitation, he said, 'you're standing on it, ducks; bloody bombs blew 'em all up.' Speechless, I continued staring at the concrete block, feeling thoroughly miserable that my efforts to find my parents had failed. Finally gathering my senses, and determined not to let this minor setback get the better of me, I began to search next for No.182 Westmoreland Road, Walworth – the place of my birth.

Taking the underground train to Stoke Newington, within a short space of time, I found myself walking along Westmoreland Road. Again, checking house numbers, I walked until reaching a long, high brick wall, at the end of which a large brick building came into view. It was No.182. Thinking it surely a mistake since I had come looking for a house, I asked a man passing by if this was the correct address. Assuring me it was, he said, 'why don't you go into reception and ask to see the Warden, I'm sure he can help you.' By this time, I thought I had missed the point, and couldn't grasp the reason why I needed to see a Warden. Mumbling my thanks to the passerby I was undecided whether to enter or run from the building. It was a formidable looking place and, instinctively, I knew it to be a place of institution. Just looking at it put fear into my heart; I felt I was about to enter the confessional box and expose my very soul.

'Truth Conquers' are words I have often heard. The truth of the matter now, was that I would never be satisfied until I knew the whole truth about myself and my parents. Convincing myself there was nothing to be afraid of, I slowly entered the building.

Approaching the clerk at the reception desk, I asked to see the person-in-charge. Offering me a seat, the young lady said, 'I'll ring and see if he's in his office.' I waited but a few minutes, when a quietly-spoken gentleman came to where I sat and introduced himself as Mr.Hewitt, the Warden. He was a slim man in his early fifties, with thinning, light brown hair on the top of his head. What struck me quite noticeably about Mr.Hewitt was not his elegant clothes or his equally elegant manners, but the majestic smile on his unlined benign face, and his small, friendly eyes which positively twinkled. He looked a 'Divine Being'. I stared at him fascinated. Although realizing he was a person of authority, I felt confident he could be entrusted with the burden of my somewhat embarrassing enquiries and I would have no qualms in talking to him about them.

Inviting me into his small office, we sat facing each other across a large oak desk on which sat stacks of papers. Asking me what he could do to help, I showed him the details of my birth certificate and asked if he held any records showing my entry into the world. Leaving his chair, he went over to a bookshelf and took from it a large, black volume. Checking the year 1925, he read out the entry – date: 25 September; time: 7.15 p.m. confirming aloud, my mother had indeed been admitted to the institution and gave birth to me on that date.

My face, no longer smug, fell flat when hearing this appalling news. It wasn't what I wanted to hear. Noting my crestfallen look, Mr.Hewitt continued, as though to cheer me up, 'you weren't the only child born here, you know; there were thousands of poor women who needed somewhere to go to have their babies, and this is where they came.' I couldn't respond to this half-cheery statement, nor minimize the hurt I felt in learning I was born in this institution. Totally depressed by the thought of it, I was determined never in my life to divulge this miserable secret to anyone.

Questioning Mr.Hewitt of any knowledge of my parents whereabouts, he responded, regrettably, he didn't know. He knew the area where they had lived quite well but with all the bombings that went on in London during the war, the majority of the people had scattered to other parts of the country; perhaps, they too, had evacuated.

Before leaving his office I questioned Mr.Hewitt about the building. He explained that the old institution was now a Geriatric Home for the Aged and was known as 'Newington Lodge'.

Apologizing for not being able to help further, Mr.Hewitt shook my hand, wished be better luck in the search of my family, and added: 'they would be proud of you.'

The Orphanage

On the return journey to Walton my thoughts trailed from Walworth to Orpington. It was here in this tiny village that I spent my childhood years – from 1927 to 1941 – living in an institution known as St.Anne's. As a child I lived in fear of those in-charge, knowing their eyes were constantly upon me. Hearing the slightest noise, a shaft of light from the nun's cubicle would cast shadows in every corner of the dormitories at St. Anne's. Silent figures, in slippered feet, carrying a lighted candle, would glide from bed to bed to see if each child was asleep. The very presence of a nun approaching a sleepless child's bed would cause her to lie there paralysed, with fright.

On November 5,1927, at two and a half years of age, I was admitted into St.Anne's, which was a large ugly-looking brick building with lots and lots of windows that looked out onto lawns and gardens. The orphanage was situated approximately twenty miles south of London and run by the Sisters of Mercy nuns, whose headquarters were located in Bermondsey. I was promptly nicknamed 'Carrie', perhaps because the nuns thought the name Catherine sounded too sophisticated for a ragamuffin like me, born in a London workhouse.

Much of my early life at the orphanage is a blur; however, I've been told that when arriving there, a strange lady took me by the hand and put me into large quarters known as 'The Nursery', which was the Receiving Home for new children. These quarters accommodated about twelve or more babies and toddlers who were cared for by the nuns and their staff. The nursery was separated from the main building of St.Anne's by a long, gravel pathway, flanked by privet hedges on both sides. Situated at the top of the pathway was the Holy Innocent Catholic church, built in 1909, through the generosity of an anonymous donor. To the right of the church was St.Anne's and to the left of the church was St.Joseph's, that housed boys from many parts of the poverty-stricken areas of London. Both St.Anne's and St.Joseph's were under the auspices of the Catholic Children's Rescue Society, and Southwark Diocese.

On the upper floor of the nursery were two little dormitories equipped with cots, a large bathroom, and sleeping quarters for the resident nun. The staff quarters were in another house, adjoining the nursery. The lower floor consisted of a dining-room with tiny tables and chairs, a kitchen, and a playroom with lots of toys and a small play slide.

Weather permitting, the children would play outside on slides and swings, under the watchful eyes of the nuns or staff. On most days, especially Sundays and feast days, the toddlers were taken for walks up the long pathway leading to the church, and taken inside to say a few prayers.

The staff, mainly young girls training to be nursery nurses, didn't stay too long at the nursery; they came and went like flies. This was in all probability due to the nun-in-charge, Sister Ethelreda, who constantly screamed at the top of her lungs, terrorizing everyone who came within inches of her. Not only did she run the nursery with an iron rod, but also the infirmary. However, it must be said that in fairness to her strong character, she was excellent in treating the children's health problems.

Although the babies and toddlers were reasonably well looked after, I was sadly aware of the lack of love they received. Indeed, I was witness to many cruelties. On one occasion, a tiny boy had wet his cot and a nurse, whose name I have long forgotten, pulled the wet sheet out from under him and beat him soundly across the legs. I was so mortified and frightened by this dreadful scene, I turned and ran crying bitterly out of the nursery and up the long pathway into the sanctuary of the church. 'Please God, I prayed, protect the children.' Looking up at the outstretched arms of the Sacred Heart of Jesus, above the altar, I puzzled how God could allow such cruelty in His midst. Sad to say no-one, not even myself, would ever think of speaking to the Mother Superior about what you witnessed, heard or felt; you simply held all your emotions tightly within and locked the secrets away, hoping that one day circumstances would change.

The nursery was to be my home until I reached the age of four, when I was then transferred to join the older girls in the main building of the orphanage and to begin my schooling. The school was within the perimeter of the children's playground and playing fields and the girls, in later years, actively participated in netball and field hockey in these areas. These games were thoroughly enjoyed by everyone, enabling us to expend our excess energies which, normally, were suppressed.

Although some of the nuns who cared for the girls under their charge were kind, most of them constantly strapped or caned us for little or no apparent reason. We often wondered why they were called 'Sisters of Mercy', because to the girls they showed not the slightest mercy, especially when exercising discipline. Ear and hair pulling went on for years, and the dread of the stinging cane can never be forgotten.

I remember clearly on one occasion, when only a youngster, accidently dropping a water glass in the refectory. I froze to the spot, petrified! I was caught by the scruff of the neck by the nun-in-charge, Sister Kevin, and told to 'go to the pantry broom cupboard, fetch a pan and brush and clean up the mess.' She then added: 'and when you've finished, girl, go and stand in the corner of the scullery and wait for me.' A few minutes later she entered the scullery holding an evil-looking cane in her hand. Looking at the cane, and knowing what was to come, I began shaking all over. Thoroughly preaching the pros and cons on being sinful, I was given three strokes of the cane on each hand. While tears fell down my cheeks, and holding my sore hands, the nun told me I was to pay for the cost of the water glass, which would be tuppence. I had no idea what tuppence looked like, or how I would find it Did God in his wisdom make the nun forget about the incident, I wondered? I never did pay for the broken glass.

Growing up in the orphanage was much the same for me as for the rest of the girls. We all dressed alike in the same navy blue serge uniforms in the winter and in the summer wore, identical striped frocks; all clothing was numbered, as you would identify prisoners. We ate the same sparse, dull meals, mainly stews, with two boiled eggs a year, one at Christmas and one at Easter, and everyone had the same distinctive convent-style of haircut, cropped above the ears. My light brown, naturally wavy hair would grow into rolls of curls which I was quite proud of. A sin in itself. To my dismay, however, the nun who looked after the girl's hairgrooming saw fit to take up a pair of heavy shearing scissors and cut the curls off, one by one. Needless to say, this action wounded my pride, and, when seeing the curls fall onto the floor, tears streamed down my face.

If a girl arrived at the orphanage at an early age which I did, she was transferred from the nursery to the infant's classroom and was taught the rudiments of early curriculum by a Scottish lady named Miss Murray, who was also the music teacher. Miss Murray was a spinster, somewhat bland and stoutly, and of medium height. She wore her black hair in a style typical of the roaring twenties, but she couldn't be described as a 'flapper' in any sense of the word as her body movements were anything but supple.

Annually at Christmas time, Miss Murray would organize the Christmas plays. A chosen few of handpicked girls played out scenes from 'The Nativity' before an audience of nuns, priests, staff, girls and visitors which included parishioners from the church. Sometimes I was chosen to play an angel, and was costumed in a white dress with transparent wings. Loudly, I would sing 'Away in a Manger', to my heart's content, totally carried away by the thought that I was floating upward to heaven. So oblivious to what was going on, on stage, I'd suddenly get a shove from one of the other players telling me to 'get on with your cue.'

Every year the play was a success. Whatever flaws there were went unnoticed, and the stage settings and costumes got better and better. Our excitement of the day was that acting before dignitaries made us feel important. Also, while normally forbidden, the players were allowed to use lipstick, facepowder and rouge on their cheeks for these occasions. This was made available to us by some of the working staff. To dream of washing off the make-up after the play would be tantamount to sacrilege; we would try making it last on our faces for days, hoping the 'importance' never wore off.

Catechism was the first priority lesson of the school day. The lessons and prayers of the Mass were taken in Latin by either the head mistress,Sister Attracta, or Father Fitzmorris, one of the priests belonging to the Holy Innocent church. What a delightful man he was; tall, slender, of delicate features and quietly-spoken, he had endless patience with any of the girls who couldn't quite master speaking in Latin. It was a sad time for everyone when God 'took him' early in his young life, and we mourned the loss. He was buried in the little cemetery, closeby the playing fields.

All children who came into the orphanage with 'questionable' baptismal records were immediately 'conditionally' baptized by the parish priest, with a staff member of the orphanage 'standing in' as Godparent.

The girls were prepared for their First Holy Communion around the age of five or six, and confirmed into the Catholic faith by the time they reached seven years. Birthdays were never celebrated at St.Anne's as the majority of the girls hardly knew the date on which they were born. The old saying, 'what you don't know, you won't miss,' certainly applied in this instance. Church was a 'must' on all holy days, and we were obliged to get up at the crack of dawn to attend mass.

Masses were also attended twice on Sundays, early and mid-morning, as well as evening Benediction. All services were spoken or sung in Latin and we chanted in parrot-style fashion our responses to the serving priest. The magnificent voices of the choir intensified the solemnity of the service, and the singing of the hymns brought me a measure of peace. Singing also provided me with the opportunity of exercising my voice box, for normally, when spoken to, we girls responded in whispered, meekly voices. This lack of voice projection affected me greatly in my early adult life as I tended to 'croak' out my words; this was not only embarrassing to me, but was annoying to the listener. I was forever being told to 'speak up.'

The joy of celebrating a feast day was made more enjoyable by the Mother Superior, who lined up the girls in the playground and, from a pail filled with sweets, would diligently dole out a few into each girl's small hand. Savouring only one sweet at a time, I would wrap up the rest of them in a piece of toilet paper or anything else I could find, and hide them in my own secret hiding place unknown to anyone else. Imagine how shocked I was, when returning one day to retrieve the remainder of the sweets, to find them all gone! Some hungry little thief had pinched them and devoured the lot, and I never did discover who she was.

By the time I reached eight years of age, I had developed much skill in the art of needlework and knitting and, on several occasions, my work was entered into competitions held by the Arts and Crafts Guild of London. Equisitite smocking, hand-stitched on the bodice of a pure, green silk baby's dress, won me a prize.

It was during this period in my life that a staff member, herself an 'old girl' told me that I had a younger sister, Elizabeth, and an older sister, Margaret, living in the orphanage. This information didn't convey much to me at the time and my response to this piece of news was somewhat negative. She collected us all together, in the playground, and pointing a finger at each of us, said, 'you, you and you, are all sisters.' Margaret was about twelve years old, with light brown, wavy hair, cut short at the ears. She looked very tall compared to me. Elizabeth was six and had dark brown, straight hair, and a chubby, little face. I cannot remember feeling any particular emotion on meeting my sisters for the first time; we simply stood staring at each other, then walked away to play with our own friends. Having a sister, what did it mean? We were also told by the same staff member that a brother of our's was living in a boy's home at Gravensend, Kent, not too far away. It would be years before any of us were to meet him.

The nuns never spoke to us about our parents or relatives regardless of whether they had knowledge of them or not; their general attitude was one of indifference. Perhaps in the mid-twenties or thirties it was the 'silent' rule. Many times, when some of the girls had parents visiting once or twice a month, I would wonder why I didn't have the same priviledge. What puzzled me was that if these girls had mothers and fathers, why were they at St.Anne's? The only parents I knew were the Mother Superior and Parish Priest, whom everyone respectfully called, 'Mother and Father'. No-one ever came to visit me.

My fondest memories of the St.Anne's girls was their profound loyalty to each other. It was a silent code never to 'snitch' on one another despite the threat of questioning or caning. If a girl got walloped by either nun or staff the other girls would rally round and comfort the victim as best as possible, offering as compensation the last sweet if you had one, or an old rag doll you made and treasured.

Not an exceptional student at school, I found it 'hard graft' coping with some of the subjects, in particular, maths. The subjects I enjoyed most were literature, history, music, arts and science and sports. Netball and field hockey I played with much enthusiasm and, excelling at netball, was chosen to play in many teams both at home and away at different schools and convents in London. It was always a thrill to be able to travel with the team and Sports Mistress by train to London, and then indulge in the delicious teas served after the match.

During my years at the orphanage, Mother Marcellina, the Superior, was the one nun whom I truly loved and respected. To me, she was the 'mother' of all mothers, and this feeling probably came about because she was always kind to all of us. Of medium height, she walked with an air of authority that made one realise she definitely was in charge. Her rosy cheeks and soft complexion gave her a healthy glow; her eyes never stopped smiling. Always scurrying here, there, and everywhere in the endless corridors or playground, her long black habit literally 'took off' in the wind and her feet almost left the ground.

Whenever entering the playground – having carefully reached the last concrete step down to the ground – the children as though appearing out of nowhere, would swamp her in greetings of love and affection. She always picked up the smallest child in the crowd, stroked her hair and kissed her, but her arms reached out to us all. She seldom reprimanded any girl unless it was something very serious.

Her punishments were usually in the form of prayers; for instance, kneeling down on the cold, marble floor under the big clock, at the top of the marble hall, and made to say six or more 'Hail Marys', with probably a 'Confiteor' thrown in. The greatest embarrassment of standing under the clock was that everyone in passing knew why you were standing or kneeling there. But, never was a word spoken.

This punishment was metered out to me twice – once when I was swinging merrily on the curtain rod in the bathroom area and it came crashing down taking most of the plaster off the wall with it; the other time when I went up to the playing field with several girls to swing on the maypole.

On this bright, sunny day, with not a cloud in the sky, we were oblivious to the fact that we were totally out of bounds and without permission of either nun or staff. The big iron rings, attached to each end of the long chains from the centre of the maypole, used to leave rustmarks on the hands and were hard to hold onto. I decided to tuck up the bottom part of my summer frock and put it through the ring, holding on only, onto the material. A girl gave us a 'starter' push, grabbed the remaining empty swinging ring and off we went, feet off the ground, flying higher and higher. We were all laughing, having a great time, when suddenly the material on my frock gave way and I was on my own, flying like a trapeze artist, over the swings and slides and landed on the other side of the field. Picking myself up, I felt somewhat shaken, but was glad of no broken bones and was unconcerned with the scratches and bruising on my arms and legs. What did concern me, though, was how I was going to account for my torn frock, now minus its bottom half. The frightening task was in reporting the damage to the workroom. We all came down from the playing field together, with the girls 'flanking' me so that no-one of authority would see the state of my frock. We walked toward to the workroom and on reaching the door, one of the girls opened it and shoved me in. I thought I was going to be sick.

Sheepishly approaching May Lyle, the school seamstress and person in charge of the workroom, I showed her my frock, holding the torn piece of material in my hand. She looked at me, unbelievingly, and her brown eyes got bigger and bigger. Shaking her finger within inches of my nose, she scolded: 'you wicked child, what have you done?' 'Take off that frock.' She handed me a pair of scissors adding: 'cut off the buttons and put them in the button box, and put that filthy torn frock into the rag bag.'

While standing in my underclothes, I was then given a clean frock and told: 'Now, go and stand under the clock and wait for 'mother.' Whoa betide you, girl, if you ever do that again.' The ordeal over, I reasoned to myself that I had got off lightly. I had half-expected a short, sharp clip around the head but mercifully, it was not forthcoming. May Lyle's nimble fingers would produce the most exquisite needlework; she was a marvel at it and every piece perfect – but if she used her strong hands to administer a wallop it could send you spinning across the workroom floor.

May Lyle taught many girls the art of cutting fabric on the bias, how to make clothes and how to knit socks on four needles. From an early age the girls were made to repair their own socks, and we sat on wooden benches in the workroom laboriously repairing the work at hand, which was carried out in complete silence as we were not allowed to speak to each other. If you did a poor job of repairing, and it was not up to May Lyle's standard, she would take her big shearing scissors, cutting out all the stitches, and make you do it all over again. A number of the girls would end up crying. But tears, no matter how bitterly shed, made no impression upon May Lyle; you did the task, even if it took all day.

There were always two rag bags kept in the workroom. One held the odd pieces of new material that came off the large rolls of fabric from which the girl's clothes were made. The other bag held odd bits of linen or clothing no longer repairable and these were used for cleaning purposes around the orphanage. When May Lyle was in a generous mood, and a girl asked her for odd pieces of material from one of the rag bags, she allowed you to take from it whatever you wanted. When making a rag doll, however, it usually ended up looking like a dressed clown, as all the arms, legs and body were made from differently textured and coloured materials; green, pink, blue, black and brown stripe. The doll's face was made from white sheeting and was stitched with strong, black thread to outline the features of the eyes, nose and mouth. Failing a thread, we used pencil.

I'm convinced that although growing up from an innocent child, a nasty streak lurked somewhere inside me, as I took the greatest delight in putting my rag doll through purgatory when testing its stress performance. Attaching the head to the body with the strong, black thread, I would twist it around and around the neck until the head was held securely in place. With a final thrust of the needle into the neck, and pulling tightly on the thread, I would complete my creation with two good knots. Then, leaving the thread attached to the doll, I would swing it crazily into the air, admiring it from every angle. Finally, when completely satisfied with my creation, I would cut it loose from its 'umbilical cord'. These rag dolls were much treasured in our younger days and we only parted with them, reluctantly, to comfort another girl.

When I was very young, Miss Condon was in charge of the workroom and May Lyle was her assistant. The two ladies sat facing each other, using electric sewing machines that stood on a wooden platform. Miss Condon had a gaunt expression that permanently masked her grey face. Her hair, also grey, was worn at the back of her head in a neat bun, held in place with long pins. She had one leg, a mystery to all of us, and a wooden crutch which she kept by the side of her sewing machine. We nicknamed her 'old woodenleg'. She never moved off her chair from the time she sat down instead, would bang the crutch on the platform and demanded: 'girl, come up here!' If questioning the girl did not produce the correct response, Miss Condon's wooden crutch – like a flash of lightening – would catch you sharply across the legs. I was totally in awe of 'old woodenleg,' and marvelled at the speed with which she could move, despite her disability.

St. Anne's Orphanage

The playground

May Lyle, our seamstress, with a group of girls

Girls on the roundabout

A gathering at Dymchurch 1938

A knitting class with Sister Attracta

Elizabeth, Margaret and Carrie
1933

Carrie and Elizabeth
Dymchurch, 1933

Carrie, Margaret, Elizabeth
1945

Carrie, age 17

One day, rumours ran riot throughout the playground that 'old woodleg' was dead. Speculating how this came about and drawing no conclusion, the girls carried on with their activites in the playground as though nothing had happened. On this particular day, I was in the workroom, when May Lyle gave me the news that Miss Condon had passed away. She then asked if I would like to see her for one last time. Rather taken aback, I muttered, 'yes, Miss.' We went up the stairs, leading from the marble hall, and walked along the upper corridor to Miss Condon's bedroom. Upon reaching the bedroom door, May Lyle ushered me in. Miss Condon was lying on the bed, with her arms folded across her chest; a bedspread had been placed over the lower part of her body. Her wooden crutch was nowhere in sight. Never having seen a dead person before I felt a bit scared and was deep in thought when May Lyle said, 'doesn't she look peaceful,' 'Yes, Miss,' I replied. After standing in silence for one minute, we paid our respects by saying one Hail Mary, for the saving of her soul, then closing the bedroom door quietly, for fear of awakening the dead, we went back downstairs into the workroom.

When I first became aware of May Lyle I noticed she had thick, white hair, and deep-set brown eyes. Of medium height, her chubby figure and motherly appearance gave her a look of one's grandmother. I noticed, also, that when she smiled, two small dimples appeared on her cheeks. She loved music and spent many hours in the workroom, long after the day's work was done, listening to her radio or gramophone records. Adept at sewing, she made many of the children's clothes and saved the Diocese thousands of pounds, sterling, in unnecessary expense. Whatever she did, was to perfection; no stitches ever fell apart at the seam on any of the garments she made.

As a seamstress in charge of the workroom she was relentless in her task to ensure that the large rolls of cloth, cut on long oak tables, were correctly cut on the bias, to avoid waste, and that any minute pieces of fabric left over, were put to good use. The rag bags taking the remaining slithers of cloth, for the girls to use when making rag dolls.

May Lyle was a devout Catholic. Daily, after eating her mid-day meal, she could be seen walking around the quadrangle in front of St.Anne's, beads in hand, saying her rosary. After walking a few circuits, perhaps not only to pray but also to exercise her limbs from sitting many hours during the day at her sewing machine, she would return to the workroom, refreshed, bodily and spiritually.

As 'children will be children', we often fell into some sort of mischief. Behind the playing fields were woods, and beyond them a farmer's apple orchards. Sometimes, when some of the older girls got into a rebellious mood, they would crawl under the barbed wire surrounding the fields and dash into the orchards to steal a few sour, green apples. The farmer would often hear the girls scrambling through the woods and breaking the branches off the trees so he would set his dogs on them. The barking of the dogs could be quite nerve-wracking because one's concentration was to steal as many apples as possible. Some of the girls who got scared would run back to the playing field with no apples at all. If this embarrassing situation occurred, you could always expect to be called 'old scarey cat' by the other girls. Those who didn't scare easily from the barking of the dogs, would tuck the apples up their knickerlegs, hoping the elastic would 'hold out' and support the fruit. Then every effort was made to run back the same way to the playing fields so as not to get caught for being out of bounds. We often found it difficult, when bending down under the barbed wire, as the bulging of the apples caused them to keep popping out of the knickerlegs and to roll all over the place. There was also risk of tearing one's clothing, hands and face, which alone pointed the accusing finger. The culprits, if caught, knew the severity of punishment and expected it. Marched off in front of the whole school, they were taken to the Mother Superior's office and reprimanded with three strokes of the cane on each hand. Tears and remorse fell in quick succession. To add fuel to the fire, the girls were then taken up to the infirmary and forced to drink a large dose of a foul liquid made from senna pods. This produced devastating effects on the intestinal system, and stomach pains raged for days. Only once did I try this foolish escapade for a dare. Caning I could almost endure, pods, no!.

In July of each year we went for a two week's camping holiday at St.Mary's Bay, Dymchurch, a seaside resort in Kent. We were packed into coaches, kit bag apiece, and holding additional clothing. Individual names and numbers were inked on tapes and sewn onto each bag – the owner being fully responsible for its contents. God help anyone who lost a garment! My number – 151 - was inked on shoes and clothing, and was also put above a tiny peg in the outside cloakroom where I hung my hat and coat. This system of numbering applied to all the girls, and often a younger girl, forgetting what number she was supposed to go by, would inadvertently take someone else's hat and coat. It was not unusual to see a small girl walk out of the cloakroom wearing a hat and coat two sizes too large for her.

Holidays were always a happy time for the girls. Once seated and counted, and being hardly out of sight of the orphanage, we would start singing with lungs to bursting point, 'Ten Green Bottles Hanging on the Wall', or 'Pack Up Your Troubles in Your Old Kit Bag and Smile', were favourite songs. By the time this jolly crowd arrived safely at the holiday camp, the singing had reached a crescendo and could be heard for miles around. The local people always knew when the orphanage kids were coming.

Accommodation at the camp comprised forty camp beds per dormitory. Each girl was expected to keep her belongings and bed neat and tidy. Older girls assisted the younger ones. Toddlers and babies did not share this priviledge and were left behind in the nursery at St.Anne's under the care of the staff.

Freedom of movement was more abundant in the mid-1930s at Dymchurch. Swimming or paddling in the sea, under the keen eyes of the nuns, and walking within certain boundaries of the camp, were permitted. Occasionally, I would stop in my tracks to admire the surrounding countryside of this beautiful Kentish resort. The salty sea air invigorated one to the point of feeling utterly carefree. To hear the wind rustling through the trees, sounding like a thousand tiny bells, the pounding of the rolling waves upon the sandy beach, alerted all my senses to the beauty of the landscape around me. Indeed, it was God's country, and only He could create such wonder.

If any girl was fortunate enough to possess a few pennies, she could go off to the tiny tuck shop nearby in the village of Dymchurch, and buy sherbet-dabs, liquorice ropes, gob-stoppers – which changed colours as you sucked them – or honey-comb bars; these were all my favourites. The only way I was able to secure money was by scanning the fields and beaches. Finding the coins I used to think how careless people were to waste money by losing it; nevertheless, when discovering the treasure, I was elated Wherever I walked, my eyes never left the ground, and never a day passed when I didn't pick up either a sixpence or a penny.

As I grew older I began to appreciate the power of a penny and what luxuries it bought, either by way of a new friend or in the form of a tasty treat. Life was becoming sweeter for me in more ways than one. I developed an awareness of my peers and quickly judged their behavioural patterns, responding to them accordingly to the benefit of my own existence. It was without fully comprehending, an exercise in the art of survival.

By the time I reached fourteen years I had finished with classroom curriculum and, as with the other girls of the same age, I was expected to work round the orphanage for the next two years, as an unpaid servant.The idea of being paid wages, was preposterous. The various household duties included the laundry, kitchen, refectory, dormitories, workroom, the nun's sitting and dining-room. Mother Superior would leave you in a job which suited you, or that you enjoyed doing. There was one job, however, I had to do many times which I must confess I resented doing, that being the scrubbing of the large refectory – all of a hundred feet long.

Every Friday evening, after the last meal of the day which consisted of bread and dripping and cocoa, four of us girls would gather in the refectory and with our gym tunics tucked inside our blue knickers, we would each take on a quarter section of the floor area. Kneeling on rubber pads, and using large buckets filled to the brim with hot soda water and scrubbing brushes, we scrubbed back to back until meeting each other in the centre of the floor. Then, turning around, we faced each other, and so as not to leave any dirty rings or tidemarks, we scrubbed the centre of the floor as hard as possible until clean.

The refectory floor was always the blackest and grittiest of all the areas in the orphanage as it was used three times daily during meal-times by hundreds of tiny tramping feet. The work took the best part of three hours and when we had finished the cleaning, the four of us would stand back proudly admiring the good, clean job we had done. We emptied the filthy water down the drain in the scullery, and then scrubbed our hands, arms and knees with large blocks of yellow soap, hoping all the dirty, slimy watermarks would come off. Our treat before retiring to bed was a mug of hot cocoa and a 'doorstep' of bread and marg.

Another duty included answering the front door. I remember clearly one particular Sunday afternoon, when the doorbell rang. I sprinted down the long, marble corridor cautiously glancing over my shoulder to see if I would be caught in the act, by a nun, of running instead of walking. I opened the big, oak door to a Mr.Hall who had called to see his two daughters. I led him into the vestibule, through to a door on the left, and into a tiny, cold marble-floored cubicle, comprising two wooden chairs. Adjoining the cubicle was a lavatory. Indicating to one of the wooden chairs in the dismal cubicle, I asked Mr.Hall to 'please sit down while I fetch your daughters.' The vestibule area had another door leading from it to the right which was called 'The Reception Room'. In comparison, this room was well-furnished, pleasantly warm and comfortable; it was reserved, however, for 'special occasions' for visiting bishops, priests and other official dignitaries, who were served tea or luncheon from the best silverware.

Having reported the visitor to the nun in the office, I ran off to the playground, spotted the two 'Hall' girls and took them back to the cubicle to visit with their father. I liked Mr.Hall. He was tall and slim, with black hair, and he always spoke kindly to me when I opened the front door to him. This Sunday, smiling, he handed me a large, red apple, which I humbly, but much embarrassed, accepted. Never had I seen an apple like this one before! Dashing back, again checking to see if I would be caught running, I went out of the door at the top end of the corridor and turned right toward the playground. Leaping up the concrete steps two at a time and oblivious to all, I began devouring this luscious treat, gouging great teethmarks into the core of the apple; the delicious juice ran all over my mouth.

Suddenly, without any warning, a voice bellowed: 'where did you get that from?' Turning swiftly around I came face to face with the head school teacher, Sister Attracta. Although a tiny nun, who always threw her black veil over her shoulder when she got angry, her voice could override that of any sergeant major's. She had a habit of lolling her head from side to side, giving the impression it would fall off at any given time during her screaming session.

Her long, black holy clothing engulfed her tiny frame and fell into thick folds from the weight of the cloth. Round her small waist was a thick strap and rosary beads, which were used in sharp contrast; one to pray with and the other to punish.The sting of the strap, whipped across my legs one day because I was caught laughing in the classroom, is an experience I have never forgotten. Sister's face was stormy. Almost choking with fright, and petrified a wallop might be in the offing, I meekly whispered: 'Mr.Hall gave it to me.' 'Be off with you, girl,' she said gruffly. I didn't have the heart to finish off the apple; my appetite gone, I tossed away the remains of it. Worried of having committed a mortal sin, and feeling the need to repent for my greed, I went into the playground. There I plonked myself down on the long, cold, hard bench and pounding my chest, whispered: 'mea culpa, mea culpa,' and asked God for his forgiveness.

Since I was now one of the older girls, Mother Marcellena, in whose presence I felt most comfortable, showed her trust and confidence in me by sending me on small errands beyond the boundaries of the orphanage. Sometimes, it would be a visit to a small chemist shop in Orpington high street, or to pick up a prescription from the local doctor's house. On other occasions I would take a parishioner's little girl, who attended catechism in the church on Saturdays, to the bus stop, and board her safely. For these tasks 'Mother' would compensate me with a coin or two, depending on the size of the task delegated. I always had to report back to her, in her small office, the minute I returned 'home.'

Clutching the pennies, farthings or halfpennies, I would take the money and tuck it into a little bag which I had made from old rag taken from the workroom, tie a knot in it and hide it safely under the mattress of my bed. I did this when I thought it was safe to do so, without the prying eyes of the nuns or girls. Faithfully, whenever earning more money I added it secretly to the rag bag, which always seemed to weigh heavy but in fact, never held more than sixpence.

I was beginning to accumulate a nice little nest-egg and felt extremely important and pleased with myself until one day, reaching beneath the mattress for the rag bag, I discovered to my horror that it wasn't there! I searched frantically for the rag bag, checking under the full length of the mattress; alas, it was nowhere to be found. Obviously, I'd been caught in the act of hiding my treasure, and someone had stolen it! I told God 'you will have to find the thief for me,' but He never did.

Undaunted, and having further earnings of farthings and pennies, I made another rag bag. However, this time I was determined, somehow, to keep it safely on my person, which was no easy task, when one was made to strip and wash in front of nuns and girls. In due course when the money accumulated to sixpence, I asked Mother Marcellena for permission to spend it in Mr.Freeman's tiny tuck shop, situated just outside the boundaries of the orphanage. You could buy all sorts of goodies with a farthing – gob-stoppers, sherbet dabs, liquorice ropes and the like – and I came 'home' with plenty of treats to share among my school friends.

During my 'in-house' training period, May Lyle entrusted me with the cleaning of her shoes – a job I enjoyed doing, for no other reason. Each week, four or five pairs of shoes would be lined up outside her bedroom door. Going along to her small room on the upper floor above the long marble corridor, I picked up the shoes and took them into the workroom where May Lyle kept the cleaning materials. According to their colour, black or cream polish was liberally applied to the shoes and I polished them until they shone like beacons.

A tiny brush, with soft rubber spikes on it, was used to gently smooth over the uppers of the suede shoes to bring up the pile. When the job was finished May Lyle would inspect the shoes very carefully and once satisfied, she would tell me to 'take the shoes and put them back outside my bedroom door.' Before leaving the workroom, she would take my hand and press into it a threepenny piece. The first time this happened I was so elated, I could have hugged her; however, such a display of emotion would never have been allowed, and could be misinterpreted, as greed. What wealth! No farthings ever came forth from May Lyle.

In 1938, I would see my last summer holiday at Dymchurch. With the outbreak of war in 1939 the camp closed, and the lovely sandy beaches were heavily barricaded with barbed wire. We all wondered what would happen to the fairground which gave us all so much fun, and the 'dolly train' which chugged right alongside the chalets and caravans on the sea front. I thought of the long summer evenings, when a number of us children would sit on the long concrete wall facing out to sea and watch, fascinated, the delightful romping and rolling of the black purpoises swimming close to the shore. The warm, red sun lit up the reeds that grew on the marshes, and would cast a magnificant glow around the sheep in the fields. We called it 'shepherds delight'.

Everyone, including the nuns, would miss Dymchurch. Memories linger of the mounds of food we devoured there in the large canteen. Breakfasts of large bowls of steaming porridge, plates of delicious, fat beef sausages with tinned tomatoes, mountains of bread and margarine, and all the milk you could drink. Dinner meals of hot stews, meat and vegetables, fish and meat pies were following by scrumptious desserts. Tea-time provided lots of bread and jam and huge slices of cake. The crowning glory of the day was more slices of delicious 'Naffy' cake – either plain or made with caraway seeds – and a hot mug of cocoa.

The holidays over, we returned to the reality of life at the orphanage looking the picture of health with tans and, of course, all packing a few more pounds of weight. Dymchurch days were happy day, never to be forgotten. We were lucky, indeed, specially during such impoverished times of the 1930s, to be given the opportunity of exploring this beautiful Kentish resort.

With the news of the war one sensed the apprehension of what was to come, and how the pattern of our lifestyle would dramatically change. The ground floor in the main building of the orphanage was turned into dormitories and if the bombing was bad during the day or night-time, nuns, staff and children crowded into the crypt under the Holy Innocent church. School lessons were disrupted by sirens that caused chaos despite repeated drills of where the girls were to go in the event if a bombing raid got under way. Mother Marcellena's main concern was always for the safety of the children, making sure rather like a hen with her brood, that they were all tucked away in the sanctuary of God's crypt.

Orpington, being very close to Biggin Hill airport – a prime enemy target – was incessantly raided. After the bombings we would find pieces of shrapnel around the school yard and playing fields but we were not, of course, allowed to keep the shrapnel or anything else we were likely to find.

One particular morning, after a noisy raid on the airport the previous night, we came out of the church crypt to find the infirmary had received a direct hit and was flattened to the ground. Debris was everywhere. This sent some of the nuns off into a panic and they scurried to see if any other part of the orphanage had been damaged. Strangely enough, as the nuns put it, 'it was the will of God that only the infirmary was bombed.' The church, hardly a few yards away from the infirmary, didn't have one damaged brick.

We often watched from the playground many aeroplanes spiralling the skies, thundering and roaring off to some foreign land or unknown battle with the enemy. We prayed daily for the young, brave pilots and hoped the war would soon be over so they could, one day, return safely home.

In 1941, Mr.R.A. Butler, then known as 'Rab' Butler became Minister of Education and was responsible for The Education Act. Educational systems began to change. This news was not well received by the headmistress of St.Anne's, who thought Mr.Butler an interferring busybody, but wouldn't say so to his face.

Changes to the girls' education were made according to the Act, regardless of whether the nuns liked it or not. The Education Act opened the door for many St.Anne's girls who had high grades and allowed them to take their exams for entry into Grammer or Commercial schools. The days of being pushed into domestic service to work, without any thought of assessing a girl's intelligence first, thank God, were seemingly over.

Rapid changes took place, and St.Anne's Orphanage became known as St.Anne's School, gradually opening its classroom doors to other Catholic children living in the area. Instead of being communally institutionalized, the girls were housed in small family units, built within the compound of the school and were supervised by one nun who was fully responsible for her charges. I was extremely pleased with this turn of event, which was long past due, and happy for those girls at St.Anne's who were now going to be brought up in a better environment. At the same time, I felt sad that these opportunities had not availed themselves to me and my friends when we were at school.

In 1941, at the age of sixteen, I was discharged from St.Anne's. May Lyle sent word for me to report to the workroom and discard my school clothes. My 'going away' outfit included a long, brown wool coat with a 'Robin Hood' style hat – feather and all, thick lyle stockings and laced-up shoes. May Lyle took a last look at me and wished me 'goodbye,' adding: 'work hard, Carrie, you'll get on well.' It was the only time I could remember her calling me by my name.

Leaving by the workroom door, I stepped inside the adjoining room which was the Reception room, and took a good look around thinking, decidedly, how warm and comfortable it was. There was no comparison between the Reception room and the tiny cubicle used for visiting parents, which was always so cold and uninviting.

I went through to the vestibule area at the front door where several of the 'old girls' were waiting to see me off. All 'puffed out', Mother Marcellena finally arrived on the scene with a staff member. She looked approvingly at my outfit and said she hoped I would do well in my job. Kissing me goodbye and thrusting a shilling piece in my hand, she said, 'keep up your religion, my child,' and disappeared behind the big, front oak door, her habit literally 'flying.'

Walking down the avenue with the staff member, I tearfully looked back at the bare, front windows of the dormitories to catch sight of several of the girls waving their goodbyes – a recognized ritual when a girl left school. I knew I would miss them. Over the years I had developed a close relationship with many of the girls in my own age group, with whom I had attended classes. We always stuck up for one another if a girl was hit by nun or staff. The consoling was very real; the loyalty profound.

Out Into the World

It never dawned on me until I went, as the nuns put it, 'out into the world,' that my upbringing was vastly different compared to that of a child who was brought up by his or her own parents. This feeling of being different from other people had disastrous effects on me in that I lacked confidence in myself. I lived in constant fear that some inquisitive mind would discover my background and the stigma of my upbringing. Like a shadow in every corner I feared images, from the past, would suddenly spring out and reveal themselves. As I was soon to learn, life in the 'outside world' was tough – there was no choice between the two evils.

The staff member and I reached Orpington railway station in time to catch the one o'clock train to London. Upon arriving at Charing Cross station, I was then transferred onto another train going southbound to West Grinstead in Sussex, and was instructed by the staff member to get off the train when it reached its destination. She told me I would be met at the station by a lady, whose name she failed to tell me. The train, crowded with soldiers carrying full packs, had no available seats and a young soldier offered me his, which I accepted. Towering above me, he started up a conversation but being so naïve, I had no idea what he was talking about. I merely sat, mute, and listened to him for most of the journey. I'm sure he must have thought, 'what a strange kid.'

Arriving at West Grinstead station I stepped down onto the platform and a middle-aged, stout, gray-haired lady approached me, inquiring: 'is that you, Miss Ashford?. She introduced herself to me as Miss Finnigan, assistant cook. Picking up my utility suitcase, we left the railway station and walked, in silence, down the long narrow country lane, lined with hawthorne hedges. Fresian cows were pasturing in a nearby field – a sight I had never seen at close quarters before – so I paused to get a closer look at them. While we were passing the farmer's gate, some of the cows went on chewing, while others simply stood glaring at us with their sad, mournful eyes. I felt an urgent desire to run and thrust open the gate and set the cows free, but the sound of Miss Finnigan's clopping shoes was like a formidable warning, telling me not to interfere with these creatures confined behind barbed wire.

Having walked well beyond three miles, we finally arrived at a large red brick building and passed through tall iron-spiked gates. Unbeknown to me at the time this was a reformatory home for boys, called, 'St.Thomas Moore', where I was to work, as a house parlourmaid, for a weekly wage of five shillings.Entering the building, a wave of despair swept over me. I couldn't grasp why I had been sent to this outlandish place which was miles from anywhere, and from the time of leaving the station, I had passed not but one soul. 'Another Prison', I thought to myself. Would there be no escaping? Little did I realize that within a matter of months I would be doing just that, as I felt I had no choice but to get away from this horrible place.

The assistant cook escorted me to an office where I was introduced to the Matron. An Irish lady of mid-years, she was petite, well-groomed, and her face had a lovely soft, pink glow. She offered me a chair and asked me several questions, to which I replied with either a 'yes' or 'no.' 'You can start your duties in the morning,' she said. 'Dorothy, the kitchen help, will show you what to do.' The interview was over.

Introductions were made to the rest of the kitchen staff by Miss Finnigan, who then led me upstairs to the attic and showed me into a tiny bedroom. 'Come down to the staff room when you're ready,' said Miss Finnigan, 'and have some tea.' Leaving me to unpack my few belongings, she retired back downstairs. I looked around the room which consisted of a single wrought-iron bedstead, a chest of drawers and a chair. Slowly, a wave of apprehension swept over me. I wanted to cry. For the first time in my life I was completely alone. I felt scared, and already missed the company of the girls at the orphanage. I went over to a small bedroom window and looked down below at well-kept lawns and colourful flower beds. The fields beyond were of lush green, and farther over more cows were pasturing in the meadow.

St.Thomas Moore was run by the Christian Brothers. Attending religious services and practicing the teachings of Catholicism were much the same there, as at St.Anne's. The hierarchy never failed to instruct me as to which of the masses, benedictions or confessions I was to attend; this routine of services never altered.

My stay at West Grinstead was a short one. The only thing I liked about the place was the surrounding countryside, which sharpened my senses to its beauty and gave me a feeling of utter peace. I could spend hours listening to the birds, and the ever-whispering of the wind in the trees, was magic to the ear. Money being scarce, and also the nearest town of Horsham being too far away, I spent my half-days off work wandering in a nearby meadow, cautiously on the look-out for farmer, bull or cows. Finding a secluded spot, hidden from view, I would sit down on the grass and count the different species of birds. Fascinated, I watched as they hopped and flew from tree to tree, unaware of my presence, and listened to their calls and songs. If I sat very still several rabbits would come sniffing nervously closeby; hares and pheasants also appearing. My idle, tranquil hours were enjoyably spent, in total oblivion to life's demands, watching nature's delightful creatures strange, uninhibited performances. Although alone in the meadow I never felt lonely; contentment and peace of mind folded over me like a warm, soft blanket.

I detested the work at the reformatory and was constantly worried of being behind schedule with my duties, which were heavy and dirty. Prior to serving breakfast to the Brothers, another duty was to clean their sitting-room and, upon entering, I would gasp for breath due to the after-effects of heavy tobacco smoking, from the night before.

I was always in a dreadful state of nervousness most of the time, causing me to drop and break things. One of the Brothers, who was short and slim with brown, curly hair, had the most piercing blue eyes I've ever seen, that frightened me. His constant gaze followed my movements everywhere and made me feel most uneasy. I couldn't comprehend this interest in me. One of my duties included cleaning his bedroom and I would dash in and out, barely flicking at the dust on the furniture, which resulted in strong complaints being made to the matron. Although sloppiness was foreign to my nature I could not give matron the reason for it, as I felt that whatever explanation I gave her, she would not have believed me.

One day, an opportunity to escape from the reformatory availed itself to me when I was accused, by the matron, of a misdeamour, causing me to become so upset that the accusing finger should have been pointed at me. With brazen nerve and courage, and without thinking of the consequences of my action, I gathered up my megre possessions and pride, and ran away. Running as fast as I could to the nearest bus stop, I boarded a Green-line bus to Horsham, and from there caught another bus going to Hove, and headed to Canon Crea's house situated on Norton Road.

Canon Crea was one of the Trustees of the Southwark Catholic Children's Rescue Society, who commuted between Sussex, Kent and London. A 'happy-go-lucky' man, he visited St.Anne's a few times a year and the girls absolutely adored him. Not very tall, a little on the rotund side, he had light, sandy colour, fine hair. Of ruddy complexion, he wore a smile from ear to ear. The affection the girls had for him was, without doubt, reciprocated by him in a genuine, caring manner. His interest was in all the children and to each one, his affection abounded.

On one of his visits to the orphanage, as he stepped down onto the concrete steps in the playground accompanied by Mother Superior, the girls, throwing caution to the wind, hugged and clung on to him tightly. His face beaming, Mother Superior unsuccessfully tried to extricate him from what seemed like the thousand arms of an octopus. I was about thirteen years old, at the time, and stood a few yards away from this merry throng, when the Canon noticed my distance and, with a finger, beckoned me towards him. Shyly approaching him, he asked what had happened to cause such red finger marks and swelling across my right eye. 'Come,' he persisted, 'tell me.'

As the chatter of the girls ceased, there was a deadly hush, and feeling all eyes upon me, I proceeded to explain to the Canon that a nun had ordered me to go down to the storeroom in the cellar and bring back a large block of yellow soap. 'Hurry, girl,' the nun had called after me. Executing an order of such urgency it was a question of whether to hop, skip or jump or run – I chose the latter, cautiously aware it was strictly forbidden within the walls of the orphanage.

Upon reaching the storeroom, which held household cleaning materials, there were other girls waiting to be served by the staff member in charge. Noting the situation and realizing that Sister's patience would wear thin if the soap was not brought to her immediately, I saw where the soap was kept on the floor and automatically bent down to pick up a slab. As I was about to get up, a staff member,

Mary Donahue, gave me a backhander across the face which stung me so much that for a minute I wondered what had hit me. The Canon listened quietly, and then saying 'goodbye' to the girls, left the playground with Mother Superior walking close behind. What transpired between them is anyone's guess, but never again did that staff member or anyone else, hit me.

Mary Donahue, along with her sisters Kathleen and Eileen, came from Ireland. All were brought up at St.Anne's from an early age. When reaching sixteen, Mary stayed on to work as a staff member, while her two sisters were sent out to work as domestic servants. As I was to evaluate later in my growing-up years, of the three sisters, Eileen appeared the most likeable and gentle. Kathleen, the eldest, only visited St.Anne's occasionally so I wasn't able to judge her fully, although whenever I saw her she always looked stern. Mary, on the other hand, had an outgoing personality who had a yen for the opposite sex, be it priest, bishop, or the Christian Brothers. She was tall and slim, and accentuated her bosom to the full, by wearing low-cut blouses. Often as kids, we would sneak to peek, to see why she chose to expose her flesh. Her strong character, and why she badly treated the girls the way she did often left me perplexed, in view of the fact that her upbringing was on the same strict principles as the rest of us. I thought, that because of this, she might have shown a little more compassion or pity when reprimanding a child, but she never did. Her punishments were as harsh as the nuns. Deep down, she may have thought that if she showed any sign of weakness in front of the nuns, they might assume a child was getting off lightly. That was not, however, how the system worked.

Mary Donahue and Sister Kevin were in charge of the refectory. From large, steel serving pots they would ladle out the food to each child holding a dinner plate, below the lip of the serving pot. If for some obscure reason Mary felt you didn't deserve the food she would crash the ladle down onto the plate, causing it to break in two pieces, splattering the food all over the countertop. The unfortunate girl would be made to clean up the mess, and go hungry. The rest of the girls waiting to be served, were shocked in silence. This episode was repeated time and time again.

"Suffer little children, come unto me", said the Lord. To suffer the stigma of birth was one thing, but to be constantly humiliated throughout childhood was another agony of sin, we all endured.

In her late thirties, Mary married the brother of one of the ladies who sang in the church choir. They had two children. The last time I saw her was on the sands at Dymchurch, in the late fifties. We passed each other, without a word spoken.

Visiting Orpington in 1984, I found that St.Anne's, St.Joseph's and the Holy Innocent church had been demolished, and that the sale of the land bought many years ago by Bishop Butt, was sold to developers for a private housing estate. No doubt, part of the deal to the developers was for them to build a small, convent house for the remaining, elderly nuns. I must confess this turn of event pleased me, as I realised, not here anyway, child abuse had slipped beneath the rubble, never to surface.

When calling at the house, I was invited in by one of the nuns whom I knew from the 'old days'. Upon entering, I recognised several statues that had been taken from the Holy Innocent church, standing in the hallway. We visited the chapel, and then I was led into the nun's sittingroom, where I noticed a nun strapped in a high-backed chair. 'Look whose come to see you, Kevin?. It's Carrie,' said the escorting nun. There was no response. Peering closer at this fragile figure, I recognised the face of Sister Kevin. She had had a severe stroke. Of all the nuns at St.Anne's, Sister Kevin had to be the most feared. Whenever I saw her approaching the playground I would run and hide behind one of the lavatory doors in the playground until I felt it was safe to come out.

I remembr her as being tall in stature, with steely blue eyes, and an aqualine nose. Her teeth that once protruded over her lower lip had now been replaced with dentures. We used to call her 'buckteeth'. No longer purposeful of stride, her white hair cut short at the ears, and her piercing blue eyes that were capable of penetrating one's soul, simply gazed into space. I looked at this once domineering nun who used to frighten the daylights out of the girls and, sadly, could not in all sincerity find it in my heart to feel any sympathy for her. While everyone attending the Centenary of the Sisters of Mercy in Orpington 1894-1994 recognised that Sister Kevin had indeed been a hard-working nun and spent most of her religious life in the service of God I cannot, however, accept that she gave any joyous service to the young children during my time at St.Anne's..

When I arrived at Canon Crea's house, I rang the doorbell which was answered by one of my dearest school friends, whom I shall name 'Theresa'. When our eyes met, the look of surprise was of disblief, and her first words uttered were: 'Gosh, what are you doing here, then? Briefly, I explained I had run away from my job. 'Oh, you'd better come in,' said Theresa, 'but God only knows what the Canon will have to say.'

When Canon Crea returned to his house, he requested I see him in his study. His conversation with me was one of kindness and understanding after I explained to him how unhappy I had been at West Grinstead. I didn't of course go into detail about the Brother who had terrorized me with his on-going gaze, as the subject was too embarrassing. On leaving his study he told me I could stay in his household for a few days and share some of the duties with his staff, who were mainly girls I knew from St.Anne's. I was happy to do this, and have the opportunity to spend a little time with old friends.

On the two Sundays I was there, Theresa and I went to mass, which then was still said in Latin. When the offering plate was passed around, I was somewhat shocked when Theresa put a penny into it and promptly took out of the plate a halfpenny. Hardly believing what I saw, I whispered to her: 'Theresa, that was terrible,' to which she replied: 'well, He's got more money than me.' I couldn't argue the fact.

I was returned to St.Anne's by train and later placed in another position in Surrey, supposedly, to look after two small children. Another disastrous situation. Not only did I take care of the children but also every cleaning job in the house. In addition, the replacement cost of every item I nervously broke was deducted from my low wages, so some weeks I ended up with but a few pennies. It seemed I was forever to be reminded of the glass I had broken in the refectory years ago which, of course, was never replaced.

War Work

In 1941, during World War Two, it was mandatory for all persons over the age of sixteen to register at the local Labour Exchange. Eager to get involved in whatever was necessary to help the war effort, also seizing the opportunity to get out of another worthless domestic situation, I registered immediately at the Banstead Exchange in Surrey and was promptly told to report for work at Vickers-Armstrong, an aircraft factory, in Weybridge, Surrey. Arriving at the factory, alongside a number of other young girls, I was given an application form to fill out, which I duly completed, to the best of my ability. After a short interview, the Welfare Officer arrived and advised me that board and lodgings had been arranged for me within a short distance from the factory.

The basic wages were low, and the only means of earning extra money was by increasing one's daily production output, for which a weekly bonus was paid. Work entailed using an electric drill for making holes in four feet long strips of metal that were used on aircraft. I didn't like the drill; it was noisy and cumbersome to hold and I was forever dropping it. Having had no prior experience in this type of work, I soon found that the industrial gloves I wore had more holes drilled into them than the metal strips. My hands were always red and scratched and the torn skin took ages to heal, due to lack of hand cream, and the cold. The shop foreman, Mr.Morrison, a short stocky man, normally so patient with his 'new recruits', was much chagrined as it seemed he was constantly replacing my holed gloves with new ones. He proceeded to show me how to get a better grip on the drill but, like a jellied eel, it continued to slither out of my hand.

The location of my lodgings, arranged through the Welfare Officer at the factory, necessitated a short bus ride to work. My tiny room, which was always bitterly cold, was in a neat, small bungalow owned by an elderly couple. Food was scarce and there was never enough to whet the appetite when served breakfast or evening meal. If meat was ever available, it was so thinly cut a sneeze would have blown it off the plate! I could hardly make ends meet; my board absorbed most of my earnings. I was overwhelmed by this new experience of poverty; it was not what I had bargained for.

Lunchtime at the factory consisted one slice of dry bread, and an oxo cube dissolved in hot water. The water was heated in a tiny metal kettle on top of a small electric ring, borrowed from one of my co-workers who used it for making tea. Meals cooked in the Work's canteen I simply couldn't afford. Not surprisely, and without doubt due to lack of sustenance, a co-worker one day found me slumped across the workbench, fortunately without the electric drill in my hand.

I was taken to the first-aid room where the Work's doctor advised a period of rest and a change of job. When returning to the factory a few weeks later, my duties became lighter and I was able to handle a sitting down job of hammering serial numbers onto aircraft components. Although the Welfare Officer managed to find me other accommodation, conditions of food or heat were no better there than the previous lodgings. Scarcity of food was even worse in this house, some days not even a slice of bread or a single potato could be found in the larder. We went to work, hungry.

Wedding Bells

At nineteen years of age, I weighed a fraction over eighty pounds and was as 'skinny as a beanpole'. In 1944, a handsome blond, in his mid-twenties, came into my life. He was nearly six feet tall. We were introduced by a friend at Walton-on-Thames, in the 'High-Spot', which was nicknamed the 'half-a-crown-hop', as this is what it cost to gain admittance. We started to court each other and within six months, we decided to get married. I had no idea that in order to undertake this ceremony, an obstacle would need to be overcome. To my consternation, I was told I would need the consent of the local magistrate as I was under the legal age and had no known parents from whom I could obtain permission to marry.

The dreaded day arrived for me to appear at Chertsey Assizes in Surrey. Feeling apprehensive, I stood before the magistrate hardly daring to breathe but, much to my surprise, the ordeal went smoother than I had anticipated. The magistrate simply wanted to know the 'why and wherefores' of who had brought me up and where I was currently living. He was kind with his questioning, and consent to marry was duly granted. Leaving the courtroom, feeling elated, I could hardly wait to give my fiance the exciting news.

The wedding date was set for July 29. Dressed in a long, white gown that I had borrowed from a co-worker namd Eileen, who was also one of my bridesmaid, the ceremony took place in the Catholic church at Walton-on-Thames. The service began at 2.00 pm and finished at exactly ten minutes past the hour.Lighted candles, mass or holy communion was forbidden due to the groom being non-catholic.

Shortly after our wedding I suggested to my husband that perhaps he might like to visit the orphanage in Kent as he had never been there. Far too embarrassed and ashamed of the stigma attached to my childhood to discuss the full details with him during our courtship, I thought he would be interested in seeing the place in which I was raised.

It wasn't, however, the first time I had been back to St.Anne's since being discharged in 1941. I tried returning, yearly, in order to meet up with some of the 'old girls' on Reunion Day, normally held mid-summer. It also provided me with an opportunity of seeking out a staff member or nun in the hope of extracting the tiniest piece of information from them about my parents. Inevitably, though, their answers to any questions were always the same: 'you don't want to know, child, let sleeping dogs lie.'

Inquiries to the Southwark Diocese in London met with no better responses; in fact, their philosophy was much worse: 'why do you want to know? We can't give you any details; we don't know.' Doors closed! It appeared as though the attitude of that era was to blame the children for the actions of their parents. The authorities and nuns treated us with unjustified contempt and referred to us as 'shameful hussies'. I could almost hear them saying this as I left their offices at 59 Westminster Bridge Road, London.

The urge of knowing my parents, and the frustration in the not-knowing, was exasperating and distressed me to the point of paranoia. I was determined that regardless of anyone wanting to help or not, I would one day find out the truth about my parents and my own identity. I wasn't to realize then, or even fully comprehend, the enormity of pain and anxiety I would suffer because of my determination to learn the truth.

My husband and I scheduled a Saturday for visiting St.Anne's and caught the early train from Walton-on-Thames to London. As was usual on the Waterloo line, uniformed men were everywhere, packed tight into the compartments. No seats were available so we stood in the corridor the full length of the journey. When the train pulled into Waterloo we managed to disembark, unscathed, before the panic of 'flying' rifles, kitbags and bodies in khaki, broke loose.

Crossing over to the Charing Cross line, we boarded a train to Kent and got off at Orpington station. Walking hand-in-hand down Station Approach road, we turned right at the bottom of it and went under a small railway bridge. A few yards along on the leftside of the road was Orpington hospital, and across on the rightside was the tall, ugly-looking building of the orphanage. I wondered how the nuns would react to my bringing a strange man into their sanctuary.

Standing near the edge of the roadside, silently staring up at this formidable grey institution, my husband piped up: 'it looks just like a prison.' I explained to him that the small, bare windows in the front of the building were the large dormitories, and that at the rear of the building the school-house, playground and the refectory could be found. We walked up the long avenue to the entrance of the orphanage, over which stood a holy statue. I told him that the big, front oak door was strictly used for important visitors. Pausing at the entrance, we decided best to enter by the church side door, which led into a small passageway. At the top of the passageway was another door that took us into the long, marble corridor. As we started walking along the corridor we noticed several nuns were coming out of the chapel area, so we stopped to speak to them. With a feeling of great pride, I introduced my husband to them. Our visit was short – unfulfilled you might say. Homeward-bound to Surrey, my husband indicated he was not impressed.

Gradually gaining confidence in myself over the years, I persisted in asking endless questions about my parents many times going back to St.Anne's and the Southwark Diocese in London. My visits, painful and very tiring, proved negative no matter to whom I spoke, be it bishop, nuns or priest. I was forced to live with their on-going philosophy of 'let sleeping dogs lie,' which of course, was not the answer. The authorities, with lips sealed, kept the doors firmly closed for forty years

Emigrate to Canada

As World War Two came to an end in 1945, I decided I would of necessity, have to go for further education if I was to secure a better lifestyle. This, I did, by going to college and taking a secretarial course. After completing the course, I then applied for a secretarial position and found that the opportunities available to me were far greater than those forced upon me, as a domestic servant, which was all the Catholic authorities were prepared to give to any girl, when leaving the orphanage.

I carried on with my career as a secretary up to the time of my daughter's birth in 1955. A year later, due to my husband being made redundant at work, he decided we should emigrate to Canada. After booking our passage we left Southampton on a rusty old Greek ship, named the "SS Columbia", an ex-troop ship, 1914, weighing seven thousand tons.

The voyage across to Canada was the most horrendous ten days of my life, and even after paying the full fare, the service we were given was shocking, to say the least! What alarmed most of the passengers more than anything was the state of the ship itself, for on going onto the boat deck and looking at the lifeboats we were appalled to find they were bolted down to the deck, so what chance of survival did we have if anything should happen to the ship. Nobody was more thankful than I to get off that floating wreck, as we docked in Wolfe's Cove, Quebec.

On arriving in Canada we journeyed to Toronto, and met up with some English friends whom we had known in the early fifties. We stayed in Ontario for two and a half years but, alas, found we couldn't adapt to the lifestyle of the big city, as we had always been used to the countryside and missed the quiet life. After much discussion my husband and I decided reluctantly, to return to England; the main reason being the oppressive heat of the summer, and the bitterly cold winters, which we could not endure.

Returning home my husband was fortunate enough to be able to secure his previous job with his old company, who were in need of a representative for the Kent area. Ironically, we found ourselves purchasing a house in the Orpington area where I was brought up as a child at St.Anne's; the memory of which still haunted me.

After settling down I decided, once more, this was an opportunity for me to carry on with the search for my family, which would enable me to go to St.Catherine's House in London and thoroughly search the records. The births, marriages and deaths records having now been transferred from Somerset House to St.Catherine's.

However, again, I seemed to draw a blank, for after travelling back and forth from Kent to the record office in London, on numerous occasions, it dawned on me that without the vital information I required concerning my parent's marriage, I would be unable to get any further ahead. Nevertheless, I was reluctant to give up my quest in the search for my family and felt compelled to explore every avenue that was open to me, on the chance that on one of my visits to the record office I would find some small item of information that would help me reach my goal.

As time passed and my regular visits to the record office became a routine and I still seemed to getting nowhere, I was most surprised to receive a letter in 1960 from a Legal Aid Officer of the Royal Naval Barracks in Portsmouth, requesting my help in obtaining a birth certificate for my brother, Harry, who was in the Navy at the time. It appeared they wanted to draft him out to a naval station abroad and couldn't do so unless he had a passport, which in turn needed his birth certificate. This was quite a shock to me, for on reflection I thought if the Navy was asking me for information concerning my brother's birth certificate, what chance would I have of getting the information I required about my family. Surely they were in a far better position to obtain information than I. Hoping it would assist my brother in getting his birth certificate, I forwarded a copy of mine to the Royal Navy. After further correspondence from the Naval Legal Aid Officer, it transpired that the details required for my brother's birth certificate were mainly taken from my own, so my hopes of gleaning any information from the Naval authorities were dashed once again.

Shortly after this episode, a further crisis occurred when the firm that employed my husband was taken over by a larger company, with the result he was made redundant, so once again he decided to uproot the family and return to Canada, hoping for a better life.

Return to Canada

After living back in England for seven years, we were rather surprised to learn from the Canadian authorities at Canada House in London that in order for us to return to Canada, we would have to re-emigrate and repeat the immigration process again. Having followed all procedures, we arrived back in Canada, April 1967; Canada's Centennial Year.

Once having settled in Ontario, we were both amazed and pleased to discover that many improvements had developed since we left in 1959. Urban development was very much on the upward swing with new plazas and housing developments springing up everywhere. The economy was booming and jobs were easy to find. I determined, that once financially stable, come what may, I would return to England at least every other year to search for any information about my family, which had eluded me so far. This I did faithfully.

It was on one of my visits to Britain, that had now become a pilgrimage, I decided to return to the orphanage in Orpington. On this particular visit in 1974, I went to see May Lyle who used to be in charge of the workroom and after sixty years of service, was now retired having reached a grand old age. She invited me into her tiny bedroom, situated on the lower floor in a small staff building close to the church, and sitting on her bed we began to chat about the 'old days'. Never without a sewing needle in her hand she showed me some beautiful silk flowers she was working on, which were exquisite and colourful. Speaking in a soft voice, she told me she knew my mother and used to watch her from her workroom windows taking her three little girls away from the orphanage, hand-in-hand down the long

57

avenue on her way back to London. She said my mother had been back and forth three times to the orphanage to take us home, and the third time the Catholic authorities called a halt and ruled: 'no more.' It was the last time she saw her children and it must have broken her poor heart to have to give you all up. She tried to keep you, she really did try.

Totally unprepared for this piece of news which came from May Lyle quite spontaneously, it not only saddened me but I was deeply shocked, because despite persistent questioning about my parents for many years everyone I approached at St.Anne's or the Catholic authorities in London, remained as tight-lipped as ever. I felt like crying! How could they do this to me and deny me information about my parents. Over the years, at the orphanage, the nuns told me I was an orphan – a 'nothing', when all the time they knew I had a mother who had visited me during my early years.

Recovering from the shock and sitting quietly for a minute or two, I then asked her if she remembered me sitting outside the workroom door listening to the music coming from her gramophone. She replied: 'yes, very well.' Leading from the marble hall were long staircases going up to the dormitories. Another staircase led down to the workroom. May Lyle obviously enjoyed music, especially the classics, and often she would take out her gramophone and play records on it, or turn on her small radio and listen to the news.

Besotted with music at an early age, I would make my way downstairs and sit as close as I could to the workroom door. My arms folded across my knees, and my head in my lap, there I would listen to the sounds coming from behind the closed door. One day, so engulfed was I listening to the music, I didn't hear the door open and May Lyle came out of the workroom and caught me sitting on the stairs. I looked up at her and shyly said: 'I like the music, Miss.' She smiled, understandingly, I thought, and went back inside the workroom, closing the door gently behind her. I'm sure she knew I often sat on the stairs many times spellbound by the music, but she never spoke one word to me; it appeared a secret bond had developed between us.

This was the last time I saw May Lyle, for whom I always held a certain affection. Of all the staff she was the only one I could remember, who often smiled. She passed away when she was well into her eighties and was buried in a small cemetry near the playing fields. Her kindness to me has never been forgotten. A great amateur photographer she took many snaps of the children as they were growing up and, but for her interest, I would not be in possession of the photographs of my sisters and me when we were young.

Life in Canada carried on as usual, and despite all my on-going visits to England in the desperate search for information regarding my parents, the doors were still firmly closed. When on a visit to St.Catherine's House in 1983, I met a Mr.Wakelin, a librarian from Hampshire, and during a discussion with him I explained the difficulties I was experiencing in tracing family records. He suggested that I write to a Lord Teviot at the House of Lords in London, as he was known to be interested in genealogy and he might be helpful to me in my search for family This I did, without delay, and although I sent Lord Teviot various pieces of information, together with a reply addressed envelope and a photograph of myself, he did not respond to my letter so once more I was disillusioned but still determined to carry on, come what may. To give up now when I had come this far, was unquestionable.

Due to my husband's poor health in 1987, he was advised by his doctor to retire from work, so we decided to move from Ontario to British Columbia, where the climate was more temperate.

When we had settled down into our new home, I was eager to search the whereabouts of the local library and found it was within proximity of where we now lived. One day, while browsing through the books on one of the shelves in the library I came across a book entitled 'In Search of your British and Irish Roots', written by Angus Baxter, an English Genealogist, living at Lakefield, Ontario. I took the book home with me and was so interested with the genealogy information contained therein, that I scrutinized every detail from cover to cover not once, but twice, determined not to overlook any knowledge that would put me on the right trail and, perhaps, open the doors which had forever been locked against me.

I resolved there and then to write to the author of the book and explain briefly how I had been searching for my parents for the past forty years, to no avail. How I had travelled from my home in Surrey up to worn-torn London, looking for any help I could get from the Catholic authorities, which was of little or no consequence. The perilous journeys I undertook travelling across London to the various record offices, having at times to make a dash for the nearest air raid shelter as the warning sounded in order to get to safety as the German bombers came droning over the capital, to drop their loads of death and destruction. All of this I was prepared to endure in my desperate quest to find my parents. Each time I approached the Catholic authorities they would come out with the same old time-worn phrase, 'let sleeping dogs lie.' I felt as though I was banging my head against a brick wall, as deep down, I had the impression that the knowledge I required was known to them but for some obsecure reason they were not willing to divulge it to me. Could it be there were answers that would rebound on them?

I pointed out in my letter to Mr.Baxter that my search over such a lengthy period of time had been fruitless, and no doubt the trail was now long cold. All I could offer him by way of documentation was a baptismal certificate which I obtained from the parish priest at the Church of the English Martyrs, where I was baptized, in Walworth, London.

After posting my letter off to him I waited in anticipation, hoping against hope I would receive a reply. As the days past I began to get anxious, wondering whether my letter to him appealing for his help had fallen on deaf ears, when out of the blue, a couple of weeks later, the long-awaited letter arrived.

Tearing open the envelope with nervous fingers, I stared at the letter dated April 12, 1988,and couldn't believe my good fortune when he stated: 'Normally – as you may imagine – I just do not have the time to do anything about personal problems such as yours – I lecture a great deal and am also in the midst of writing another book and six articles a year for 'Heritage Quest.' However, every now and then someone gives me a problem which touches my hard heart and yours is such a one. I will do all I can to help you.' He then went on to listing various questions about my parents, my history before I was nineteen, and to sit down, rack your brains, give me the answers to my questions, send me a copy of your birth certificate if you have one. Tell me the exact date in 1925 when you were born and tell me how you know this. He added: 'I can understand your frustration and will do all I can to help – but I have no magic touch and may not discover any more than you.'

In response to Mr.Baxter's letter I endeavoured to answer his questions as best as possible, and enclosed my brother and sisters' birth certificate, along with my own, hoping they would be of some help to him. It was impossible for me to give him any details of my parent's background, as I simply had no knowledge of them whatsoever.

In Mr.Baxter's following letter dated June 6, 1988, his opening remarks were that he had nothing positive to report. He had visited England in May 1988, for four weeks, and had spent hours at the headquarters of The Society of Genealogists in London checking through directories for the whole of London for the period of 1918-1930 for any record of my parents as either owners or tenants of a house or apartment. There were none.

Mr.Baxter's next visit was to The Public Record Office in Kew, Surrey, where he spent the day searching through naval records for my father, but found nothing positive. He then decided to put certain enquiries in motion; a search of London's Poor Law records for the Walworth area; a record of naval enlistment of my father since 1891, whether he was a regular sailor, or whether he was a stoker during the 1914-1918 war; a check by a contact of his at St.Catherine's House on the birth of either of my parents in the period 1880-1890. In fairness, he could not ask for a longer search at this stage. We will see what comes out of these enquiries.

After further correspondence with Mr.Baxter, who had been so generous in giving freely his invaluable time on my behalf, the floodgates finally opened, and through his contacts in England I received information about my father who had served as a Chief Petty Officer in the Royal Navy, along with his service record dating back to 1902, from the Ministry of Defence in Hayes, Middlesex.

As the New Year of 1989 approached I felt something positive would be happening and in due course on January 24, I received news from a Mr.Rudall (Mr.Baxter's contact in London) that he was sending my parents' birth and marriage certificates to me. Overcome with emotion, I knew at long last all the journeys, the hardship and anguish suffered by me, were worthwhile.

Elated at my good fortune in receiving this news of my parents, I decided to make another journey from British Columbia to England as I was more eager than ever to see the tiny village of Lydd in Kent, the birthplace of my father.

I didn't realize at the time that this undertaking would, at some later date, bring the most astounding news, along with the biggest surprise of my life.

Arranging my flight to the UK, I duly landed at Gatewick airport, to be met there by my brother, Harry, whereupon we took a taxi to his home in Hampshire, travelling through some of the most beautiful countryside of southern England. After settling down at my brother's house, we discussed our plans to visit various places of interest to us, in particular father's birthplace in Lydd.

In response to previous letters written by Angus Baxter to the Chatham, Rochester and Gillingham News, the Kent Evening Post, and the local newspaper, Lydd, making a general enquiry on the subject of ancestor hunting, mentioning only my father's name, place of origin and naval service, we were put in touch with a second cousin who had apparently, as a child, while her father was serving in the Army during the Second World War, lived with my grandfather Edward Rutley Ashford, in Lydd, Kent, with her mother, brother and sister. This family were totally unaware of my existence. My cousin whose name is Wendy, and lives in Bexhill, kindly offered to show my brother and I around the village of Lydd as she knew the area well, when living with grandfather. Meeting up with her the following day, we were taken to this delightful little village and through the lovely old Saxon church, parts of which date back to 1557. It was here that we were shown the graves of some of our ancestors, among whom was a Lieutenant J.D.Godfrey, R.N. DSO. of the HMS "Arethusa" who during the Battle of Helegoland Bight in World War One, was credited with firing the torpedo that sank the German Battleship "Blucher." For this, he was awarded the Distinguished Service Cross.

While travelling around Lydd with my cousin and brother we were introduced to the Parochial Secretary of the Church, a lady by the name of Dorothy Teck, who at that time was in the process of working on the Ashford family tree. This timely event came about because her husband's friend was related to the Ashford's of Lydd and requested this favour from her. After a lengthy discussion on the family's history it was too apparent, to both paries, that the information we had exchanged was startling, to say the least! On the Ashford tree, there was no indication that my father had any children, according to Dorothy Teck's records. Before taking our leave, Mrs Teck put me in touch with a David Wilks, a researcher in family history, living in Whitstable, Kent, saying: 'I'm sure he will help you.'

Seizing this opportunity, I wrote to David Wilks asking if he could possibly obtain my mother's death certificate for me, which was a problem due to the fact that I could not provide St.Catherine's House in London with the date or year in which she died.When requesting this piece of information from David Wilks I had no idea of the repercussions that were to follow, leading me to the one person who was to give me all the news I wanted to hear concerning my mother. Although I was anxious for these details, I could not but help think that all the years I had been searching for her the nagging feeling of why she allowed my sisters, brother and I to be put into an orphanage without seemingly any thought for us, did not lessen my grief as to the reasoning for this sad episode in my life.

The time passed all too quickly for me as my holiday in England ended, and so I returned to my home in Canada satisfied with what I had accomplished. March 1989, while unpacking my luggage the following day, I came across the envelope that Dorothy Teck had given me, with the address of David Wilks, and thought it would be an opportune time to write to him to see if he could unravel any of the mystery that surrounded my family. Up to this time, inspite of searching for over forty years, all I had managed to obtain thus far was my parents' birth and marriage documents, so I requested him to search the records to find any information he could on my mother, in particular I was desperate to secure her death certificate. This, I knew, would enable me to see in which part of England she lived at the time of her death, and where she was buried.

As the days lengthened into weeks and there was no correspondence from Mr.Wilks, I began to get extremely anxious and the thought struck me, that being so many thousands of miles away, literally across the other side of the world, it was a case of 'out of sight, out of mind.' Feeling rather despondent, I toyed with the idea of telephoning my brother in Hampshire to see if he could help as far as inquiring from Mr.Wilks but, on second thought, discretion being the better part of valour, I decided against this move. However desperate I was to press on ahead with my search, I decided to wait and see.

A month later, patience it seems, paid off for me, as a week later on taking the mail from the box there to my relief and joy was the letter I had long awaited from David Wilks. Thanking me for my letter, he apologized for being so long-winded in replying, due to pressure of work, then without further ado got right down to business by requesting a fee of one hundred and twenty-five pounds, sterling, for a two-day search for my mother's death certificate, providing I forward him her birth and marriage documents, which I had successfully obtained through Mr.Rudall in London.

My father's death certificate was made possible through the kindness of Angus Baxter, when he had advertised in the Chatham, Rochester and Gillingham News, which was responded to by a Mr.Cyril Scott who lived at Strood, Rochester. In Mr.Scott's letter to Angus Baxter, he stated he knew my father, since a boy of eleven, as Ted Ashford and that Mr.Ashford had worked at the Royal Naval Barracks, Chatham, since leaving the service. He went on to say that my father had been dead for many years and his wife Sarah went to live in Devonport, Plymouth. Mr.Scott's closing comments were: 'as far as I am aware, Ted Ashford had no children.'

In thanking Mr.Scott for providing me with this valuable information, I let the matter rest there. However, a week or two later I was dumbfounded to receive another letter from him, enclosing a certified copy of my father's death certificate, which I had not requested of him. He must have sensed the urgency in my previous letter for information of my father, as he took it upon himself to write to the Register of Births, Deaths and Marriages, Chatham, Kent, for this document, enclosing the required fee of five pounds, sterling.

It is not necessary for me to relate what it meant to me in receiving this certificate, which a complete stranger had taken it in his heart to achieve on my behalf, but if I had only met someone like Cyril Scott years ago when searching for my parents, my ordeals would surely have been minimized. Sadly, when visiting England in 1989, I made a special journey to see Cyril Scott at Strood, Rochester, as I personally wanted to shake his hand and thank him for going to the trouble of getting my father's death certificate, but upon calling at his house I was informed by his wife, May, that he had passed away a few weeks earlier.

In June 1989, at last, the news I had waited for arrived as with the next letter from David Wilks, he enclosed my mother's death certificate along with a copy of my father's Will, which I had not asked for. Together with these documents I was surprised to see another death certificate for my mother's fourth husband, a Thomas Marsden, whose marriage to my mother in 1928 had been confirmed earlier by Mr.Rudall but the 'sting in the tail,' was a further request by Mr.Wilks, for an additional seventy-five pounds, sterling, to cover extended labour hours. In reply to Mr.Wilks, I thanked him for his excellent work in furnishing me with all these documents.

Having already secured details of my father's naval records from the Ministry of Defence, Hayes, Middlesex, and family history of the Ashfords from Dorothy Teck, the Parochial Secretary of All Saints Church, Lydd, Kent, I resolved to persue mother's side of the family hoping this would satisfy the anguish, heartache and pain that lay within me for the past forty odd years. Perhaps it would finally give me peace of mind in the knowledge that I had family. And I really was someone and not just a piece of flotsam as the Catholic authorities would have me, drifting along on the ocean of life.

In my letter to Mr.Wilks, I asked him to search the Adams side of my family; this being the maiden name of my mother. Having mailed this off to him, I sat back quite pleased with myself, thinking it might eventually clear my last obstacle and that I was heading for the final chapter in my desperate quest for family history.

Having received a further letter from Mr.Wilks dated July 2,1990, he stated: 'the details about your parents and brother and sisters, according to the photocopies, are indeed complex and mystifying at this stage.'To start investigations would require three or four days work; the initial fee to cover these costs, would be two hundred pounds, sterling. My reply to Mr.Wilks was to request that he go ahead with the search, realizing what a formidable task I had placed before him.

It would be September 10, 1990, before receiving news from Mr.Wilks, and to be quite frank I didn't expect to hear too much concerning the Adams, as they seemed to have disappeared. Hastily opening the envelope, I withdrew from it four sheets of correspondence and in so doing, a folded document dropped out. Thinking this may relate to mother's family, I ignored it for the moment and continued to read the enclosed letter.

Suddenly, I stood transfixed and rooted to the spot. I couldn't believe what I had just read, it seemed preposterous. In his letter David Wilks stated: 'when checking for the Adams family, he drew a blank, so decided to try another avenue of search on the Ashford file, mother's married name. After a final and colossal search he came up with the following birth index for a Charles G.Ashford born in London, January, 1919. This person appears to be a full and legitimate brother to yourself. Prolonged investigation may reveal his present whereabouts, and that I am sure will lead to verbal proof of the background of your childhood. So I imagine that if Charles G.Ashford is still alive, and can be traced, he may be able to say much more than we are able to surmise from documentary records, such as his birth certificate that I have forwarded to you.'

Regaining my composure after reading such astounding news, I hurriedly put on my coat, got into my car and drove over to my daughter's house which was a short distance away, to show her the letter. Upon arrival, she took one look at me and said: 'mother, what's up?' I could hardly contain myself, as I handed the letter to her, saying: 'you won't believe it.' Sitting down, I watched the expression on her face as her head moved from side to side while she read each line carefully. Then, with a look of utter amazement spread.over her face, she gasped: 'it's not possible, it's so unreal, do you think someone is playing a joke on you, knowing you are constantly in search for family?' In response to her question, I withdrew my brother's birth certificate from the envelope, saying: 'I don't think anyone would go to the trouble of forging an official document for a joke, do you?' To say we were ecstatic, is to say the least! My excitement knew no bounds in the news that I had found a brother, whose existence was totally unknown to me. I wondered, could he be alive, or am I too late, because of his age. He could be long dead, or maybe killed during the last war. All these possibilities were uppermost in my thoughts, nevertheless, I decided to press on; the road had been too hard and long for me to stop now.

Without further delay I wrote to Joan Swale, a friend of mine who lives in Lydd, Kent, telling her my wonderful news I had received from David Wilks, who had found a brother by sheer luck when checking the Ashford birth indexes at St.Catherine's House in London. I mentioned in my letter to Joan that a further fee of two hundred and fifty pounds, sterling, would need to be paid if I wanted Charles's whereabouts known to me. In the light of this and the fact he would be seventy-two years of age at the time of writing, also he could be long gone, did she think it worthwhile persuing this course of action or could she advise me on the best way to go about obtaining this information. The fact that Joan herself was extemely involved and interested in genealogy and had many successes over the years in tracing her own ancestors as well as her friends and other people who wrote to her for help, I was sure her advice on my efforts to find Charles would be sound and prove positive.

I didn't have to wait long for Joan's reply. She suggested the best way to handle this without too much expense involved, would be to write directly to the Salvation Army Headquarters in London whose successful work in tracing missing relatives was known throughout the world. Joan went on to say that whatever particulars I had on my brother, plus a copy of his birth certificate, that I forward these on to them. By the way, she added: 'don't forget to send them a donation as the work they undertake is for a worthy cause.' Taking my friend's advice, I wasted no time in posting a letter off to the Salvation Army, pleading for their help. This I hoped, would at least give me the vital news I so badly wanted, informing me of the whereabouts of a brother I had never known.

As the days passed into weeks and lengthened into months, and time slowly dragged on, I began to wonder if I would ever get any response to my plea for help from the Salvation Army. After almost three months had gone by and Christmas was drawing ever nearer, I busied myself sending off greeting cards to my friends and relations overseas. One day, on picking up my letters from the mail box, I was surprised to find a letter addressed to me with a Liverpool postmark on the envelope. Rather puzzled, I thought to myself who do I know from that part of England, the only time I saw Liverpool was when I joined a ship there, to emigrate to Canada in 1967, aboard the 'Empress of Canada'.

Opening up the envelope I withdraw a Christmas card from inside and stared at the message on the front of it which said: 'To a Wonderful Sister'. I had already received a card from my brother Harry in Hampshire and, rather puzzled, I thought I had someone else's mail, but on opening out the card I read, 'from your loving brother, Charles.' Trembling with excitement, I stared at the card in my hand and knew, without doubt, it was positive proof that he was alive. Although the hand-writing was nervously scrawled, I could detect from it strokes of characteristics similar to those of my own. Turning to the enclosed letter I slowly read the address, hoping there would be a telephone number to enable me to make contact with him; alas, there was none. Picking up my telephone directory I called the overseas operator in England to see if Charles was listed in the Merseyside 'phone book, but the operator informed me there was no such listing for a Charles G.Ashford; however, he added: 'his number could be ex-directory.'

Determined not to waste any precious time, overjoyed as I was at receiving a beautiful Christmas card from

Charles, I 'phoned Harry in Hampshire to tell him I had heard from Charles, whereupon Harry asked if I would let him have his address so he could write to him immediately. Christmas was but a couple of days away and, as was usual, my sisters Elizbeth from Victoria and Margaret from Washington State, came to spend the holiday with me. It was always a great time for us to spend Christmas together, along with my daughter and her family, and enjoy the festive season with lots of lovely gifts, the trimmings off a fat turkey and homemade Christmas puddings. This was the one meal of the year we savoured and laboured over for hours between the chatting and laughter. These Christmas get togethers were a joy to us all – we were family and that's all that mattered!

As the New Day of 1991 dawned I awoke to find we had all slept rather late into the morning, no doubt due to celebrating the festive season. The breakfast hour had long passed so I prepared a light lunch, hoping everyone would be fit enough to partake in the meal. We all went into the dining-room and as we sat dining the noise of the telephone ringing cut short our chatter. Rising from my chair at the table, I glanced at the clock on the wall, which indicated one o'clock. I wondered who on earth this could be as we had already spoken to our many friends previously. Picking up the receiver I said: 'hello'. The reply I heard all but threw me off balance, as a voice answered, 'hello Catherine, this is your brother Charles.' I couldn't believe my ears, I was so overwhelmed on hearing his voice for the first time that when I tried to speak the words just stuck in my throat. I called out to my sisters in the dining-room that Charles was on the 'phone, and as their heads looked towards me the look of utter amazement on both faces made me want to burst out laughing; their eyes popped out like organ stops, they were that surprised!

We chatted, excitedly, for a good half hour, trying to cram in the questions of a lifetime. I then handed the 'phone over to my sisters, so they could chat with him. Finally, after promising he would call again soon, we all wished him a Happy New Year, he returned the compliment, and reluctantly rang off. Not wishing to replace the receiver, I held on until I heard a faint click of the line being switched off by the operator, and a wave of deep emotion welled up within, bringing forth a flood of tears. On turning to face my sisters I found that they also had been overcome by the surprise telephone call from Charles. While chatting together, we wondered how our newly-found brother had fared throughout his life. He had already told me, briefly, in our telephone conversation that he had lived with our mother from the age of thirteen until joining the Merchant Service and embarking on a sea career at the age of seventeen. To hear that he had actually lived with mother for that period of his life, while the rest of us were pushed to one side, brought a feeling of great sadness to us all. I asked myself, 'why did Charles go home, and not us?' This question continued to haunt me, and as the months dragged by and our correspondence to each other became like a flood tide, I would try and glean as much information as possible from Charles regarding our mother.

At this stage, however, he was trying to get over the loss of his wife to whom he had been married for forty-six happy years, and passed away the previous August. Although finding me was a miracle which he never expected would happen to him in his lifetime, it was difficult for him to come to terms with his tragic loss. He was also proccupied with the sale of his house, a most unpleasant task for him to undertake, and taking all these facts into consideration I felt it would be kinder if I didn't push too hard for the vital information I needed, and allow him to relate his story to me in his own good time. We had already made plans for him to come and stay with me in Canada for three months, when the time suited him, but nevertheless I felt an urge driving me on, to lift the veil of secrecy that hung like a huge dark cloud over my life.

Eager for any tiny morsel of news about mother, in further correspondence between us, I couldn't resist mentioning that she had remarried and to all intents and purpose, abandoned us. In his letter, replying to my questions, Charles said he too failed to understand mother's lack of parental care for her children but, then, we should not judge her too harshly as times were very hard for young women in that period and her circumstances are unknown to us, so who are we to stand in judgement of her. Scant as the facts are concerning mother, it must have been painful for her to relive the past. In conveying my thoughts, it might be better if I put the words into prose. Stemming the tears that threatened to cascade all over the paper, I slowly read the poem Charles had sent me, and I marvelled at the explicit way in which he wrote each verse trying, in the kindest possible way, to see mother's plight.

Having now contacted first cousins on father's side of the family in Lydd, Kent, it was difficult to understand why they were unaware of my mother's marriage in 1915 to their Uncle Ted, and were shocked to learn he had children. As far as they knew he had no direct family, being married late in life to a widow in 1928.

Time moved slowly forward, as I counted each day anxiously awaiting to meet my brother, for the first time. In the meantime the correspondence and telephone calls continued at a startling speed, each time praying for more news of Charles's past life. All he would say was he had a reasonable childhood, only to face a rather tough period surviving World War Two.

Eventually, the call I longed for, came in late July 1991. His message was short and to the point, as he told me in a voice filled with excitement: 'Catherine, I have sold my house, and have booked a flight, arriving Victoria airport at 3 pm. July 31, see you soon.'

I glanced at the calender hanging in the kitchen. It was the 28. My head began to spin, I felt so happy, three days, I said to myself over and over again, it was so hard to believe, at long last, after all the years of frustration, and lies from the authorities, I would come face to face with a brother whose existence was unknown to me, and was the one person who could provide me with reliable news of my mother.

The longest three days of my life were about to end, as I made preparations for Charles's arrival. How I managed to get through lunch that day, I'll never know. Needless to say, I arrived at Victoria airport long before the plane was due, and proceeded to walk up and down impatiently, watching the hands of the clock, as they slowly moved to 3 pm. Looking at the arrival screen and noting the plane was due, I made a beeline for the window just in time to watch the tiny island plane with its precious cargo touch down on the tarmac. Waiting for the arrival doors to slide apart, I eagerly scanned all the faces of people coming out. Suddenly, there he was, my newly-found brother, and leaving his luggage he rushed over to me with arms outstretched. As we hugged each other, he whispered: 'this is the moment I have longed for all my life.' In a voice choked with emotion, and holding back the tears, I said: 'miracles do happen.'

The three months Charles and I spent together, will be memories treasured forever. On most days we visited the numerous beautiful coves and beaches in and around Victoria, as well as other places of interest, which we enjoyed. In the light of the warm summer evening we would go for long walks on the beach, resting a while on a log facing out to sea, and chat about our family, in particular mother. I couldn't fill my insatiable appetite for every scrap of news Charles had of her; I wanted to hear the details now, rather than at some later date, knowing at this stage of my life, time was of the essence.

I told him of the hardships I had gone through in my younger days, my early marriage, finally emigrating to Canada, seeking for a better life. Listening quietly to me, then speaking in a soft voice, he said: 'it's so sad that we didn't find each other years ago, as I could have made your life so much easier.'

Before returning home to England, Charles and I agreed we would each write our own story, initially, I suppose, and for want of a better phrase – to 'expose our souls'. So much, in the past, has for one reason or the other, had to be concealed. My one fear, when going 'out into the world,' as the nuns so aptly put it, was the dread of some inquisitive mind finding out the stigma attached to my childhood background. It was a fear so deeply rooted it wasn't until the year 1990, that I could bring myself to utter one word of my background to the person most dear to me, my daughter. It took all my courage to give her the details of my life, from the beginning, and when I had finished, it was as though that solid, block on concrete I stared down on in the East End of London in 1944, had been lifted off me. Getting it out of my system, left me exhausted.

My daughter told me she always felt there was a certain mystery surrounding me, as I never spoke of my family; however, what she had just heard, neither surprised or shocked her.

Full Circle

If someone was to ask the question: knowing what you know today, would you do it all over again, my answer would have to be 'yes.' The drive to know my roots was so intense I was determined, regardless of whatever hurdles I had to cross, I was not prepared to let anyone or anything stand in my way.

Had I been aware of The Society of Genealogists headquarters in London when I began my search in 1944, I'm sure I would not have travelled trails, long cold, in all the wrong places. The back and forth exhausting journeys to the East End of London left me physically drained, and I wondered many times if I would have the strength to continue, alone, the search for my parents. Often, walking many miles through bombed-out London, I would stop to rest, sitting on a pile of debris, with dust and dirt everywhere. If lucky enough to be able to purchase a piece of fruit from a barrow boy, this I considered was lunch; the only food I ate throughout the day.

As far as the Catholic authorities were concerned, I should not have wasted my time in trying to extract from them information; the 'silent rule' prevailed, no matter what! It is only now that those people who were put under their charge, as children, have found the information that they searched for. Sadly, for many of us it has come all too late, and has caused needless misery to those who have lived a lifetime, alone, and without family.

In a letter from Mr.M.Lyons of the Catholic Children's Society in Purley, Surrey, dated June 14,1993, I quote: 'Yes, it is sad that it has taken so long for people like yourself to locate families. It is really only since 1976 when adoption records were opened up for the first time that it had become so evident to everyone, how important family records are. The expertise in tracing is fairly recent and we have learned so much in recent years about what is available, where to look, and how to 'prise' information out of the archives of long defunct Agencies.

As you have already gathered, there was no co-ordinated Welfare Service for children, much before the 1950s and certainly few professionally trained people with any knowledge of child development or needs. The old orphanages just provided the basic minimum in shelter, food, clothing and education but could not by the very nature of the institutions provide anything in the way of real individual love or meet the individual emotional needs of young children. Even today the authorities are 'struggling' to find answers to complex questions of why some families survive and others cannot cope.'

Throughout my correspondence with Mr.Lyons, going back to October 1988, I must say in all honesty that in all my inquiries concerning my childhood background, he has made a thorough search of the records, currently held at Purley, Surrey, England, and given me details that were perhaps useful or beneficial to me, relating to my two sisters and myself. There was, however, one letter I received from him dated September 11,1989, which was in response to an inquiry concerning my brother, Harry, who had been put under the care of the Sisters of Charity nuns at Gravensend in Kent.

After searching, he had eventually found an entry in an old register held at St.Mary's, but it gave little knowledge, other than the date he was admitted, his first Communion, Confirmation, and when discharged. There was, however, a piece of information which both Harry and I were totally unaware of, up to this time, and I was so angry when reading these details, I could have exploded: 'Nearest relative mother, Caroline, 105 Albany Flats, Albany Road,

Peckham.A notation across this line read: 'this is then crossed through and underneath is written.' The address was No.72 Westminister Bridge Road, London, SE1. It was, without doubt, an appalling thing for the Catholic authorities to do, after begging them to give us any details, however small, to enable us to find mother. For years they kept this vital piece of information to themselves, saying repeatedly, 'we don't know.'

Having come full circle, and realising a goal which appeared insurmountable, I can now look back on the past forty years as being the most challenging experience of my life. I have met many people willing to help a complete stranger in the smallest way, and when travelling around the East End of London, exploring dark, narrow corners, which terrified me, I found the Cockney, East Ender, the most warm-hearted, endearing characters of them all. The information as to how I could get to a specific area, the Catholic Church of the English Martyrs, or other areas of Walworth, when asking for information, a Cockney would sometimes go out of his way and take me directly to the place where I was heading, chatting all the way, and laughing in his good-humourous manner, that only a Cockney knows best.

My roots, now firmly established, have come about through the generosity of Angus Baxter, who gave me his invaluable time and advice so freely on where, or how to go about extracting information from the various Record Offices and Government departments in England. To him I owe a debt so great, it can never be repaid. But for the doors he 'opened' it would have been an impossible task for me to secure my father's service records from the Ministry of Defence, also my parent's birth, marriage and death certificates through Mr.Rudall, his contact in London. Unfortunately, I have not had the good fortune to thank Mr.Baxter personally for his many kindnesses, understanding and encouragement. Perhaps there will come a time soon, I hope, when I can meet him and shake his hand.

My greatest joy when Mr.Baxter wrote telling me that he had found my family, was that once contact had been made with them, family photographs were made available to me. I was, of course, delighted with these, especially those of my father in his Navy uniform. And what a handsome man he was. I don't doubt my mother fell 'hook, line and sinker', for him. Throughout the course of my search for roots, whatever information became known to me, along with any photographs I was able to extract from living relatives, all these documents were forwarded to my brother Harry and sisters, Margaret and Elizabeth, so they were kept completely uptodate with current news and progress.

Charles, our eldest brother, has now taken over the reins from me in furthering our search for mother's side of the family, the Adams, and has been successful in making connection with mother's niece, Betty, who lives in Sussex, and informs us that she has been working on the Adams family tree the past thirty years. June 1993, I received a letter from Betty enclosing numerous photographs of my ancestors; one of my mother at age twenty-two. The information my cousin has compiled over the years is incredulous. Grandmother Adams had seven daughters, four sons, two of whom died at a very young age. These children have, unfortunately, all passed on. Uncle Ernest, one of my mother's brothers, whom I had been trying to trace this past two years, with information obtained at that time, passed away February,1989. His wife May, died in 1992.

Of the children of my uncles and aunts, some live in Australia, New Zealand, Quebec Canada, and England. There is some mystery attached to my aunt Lilian Adams and her second husband, John O'Connor, whose child Marie O'Connor was also born at 182 Westmoreland Road,

Walworth, and appears to have been taken to Canada by her father many years ago. The past thirty years have been spent trying to trace her whereabouts, to no avail.

My brother Harry lives, alone, in Hampshire after losing his lovely wife, Olive, some years ago. He served in the Royal Navy for twenty-seven years and is retired on a Navy pension. With three grown-up children, the eldest son living in Ontario, Canada. Harry has eight grandchildren.

Margaret married a young soldier named William Evans, who served in the Canadian Army during World War Two. In 1947 she sailed to Canada, with other war brides, and lived with her husband in Quebec. A young child was born to them; however, sadly, the baby died of a crib death. To add further to her anguish, her husband was drowned a few days later. Such a tragedy, which I'm sure my sister never got over. After many years of struggling to maintain herself in Canada she decided to emigrate to the States, but her life here was far from easy. Her love of animals far exceeds that of the human race. Despite the extreme hardships Margaret has endured throughout her life, she can still come up smiling. Like the rest of us, she is a true survivor. Elizabeth, my younger sister, a most endearing, loving person who wouldn't hurt a living thing, over a lifetime of looking after the young, old and sick, was hanging on to life by a thread before passing away in 1993. Her death left an enormous gap in my life. We were sisters and close friends and I loved her dearly. A devout Catholic she never questioned the church's theology, and stood by her faith, resolutely.

Of all the frustrations throughout my search for family, the one 'fly in the ointment' has to be John Brandon, an Irishman, who was one of mother's four husbands. He was born in Dublin in 1890. On July 4, 1910, he joined the Royal Navy as a Stoker II Class on a 12 year engagement.

His Office Service Number was K.7335, Port Division Portsmouth.

He was released ashore, HMS Victory II, on July 3,1922, the period of his continuous service having expired. He joined the Royal Fleet Reserve on October 20, 1924, Official Number Portsmouth B.15566. In a letter from the Ministry of Defence dated July 10,1991 responding to an inquiry on Brandon's service records, it stated: 'we have established that he was released from the Royal Fleet Reserve in November, 1932, and we have every confidence that he did not serve in the Royal Navy during World War II; certainly he did not die on active service with the Royal Navy during that conflict. Further research has shown that, whilst his service record gives his previous occupation as 'Ship Fitters Mate,' his engagement papers show him to have been a 'Farm Labourer.' Which is odd, and that he had previously served with the 3rd Battalion, Scottish Rifles (Special Reserve), although he enlised in the Royal Navy in Belfast..

In a further letter dated September 30,1991 from the Ministry of Defence.I quote: 'in reply to your enquiry, we regret that no records relating to the Military service, of 40123 Peter John Brandon or JOHN Brandon -Scottish Rifles, in the British Army during the 1914-18 war can now be traced.Unfortunately, as was mentioned in our original letter, a large proportion of the records of soldiers who served during the period 1914-20 were totally destroyed by enemy air action in 1940 and it would seem that those of the above named were among them.'

My letter of June 2,1992, to The Cameronians (Scottish Rifles), Chester, England, their response was negative, but they did furnish me with some background information relating to this battalion, which I found most interesting: 'The 3rd Special Reserve Battalion came into being as a consequence of Lord Haldane's Army reforms of 1908.

During the Great War the battalion was mobilized and was sent to Nigg in Ross-shire, Scotland, where it remained until 1918 when it proceeded to Invergordon, and the following year to Bridge of Allan. When trouble in Ireland became acute the Battalion moved to Curragh. It may be that during their stay there, your relative left the Regiment and joined the Royal Navy.'

Because of the destruction of records in Dublin in 1922, it is impossible to secure the birth certificate of John Brandon.. The one record I have relating to him is the marriage certificate of December 17,1919 when he and my mother married in a London Registry Office. Even this document is suspiciously questionable.

My father was cremated at Charing, Kent, in January 1958. My mother passed away at age sixty-four with cancer and was consecrated at St.John's Cemetery, Margaret, Kent, April 1952. Ironically, my sister Elizabeth had worked in this area in the 1950s, never realising how close she was to her mother. When Charles and I visited mother's grave in 1992 it was on a bitterly cold day, and as we walked from the railway station along the beach front the wind and rain howled across from the ocean, causing large waves to splash unmercifully over the shortline. We stayed by the graveside for a few minutes, deep in thought, that perhaps life might be been so different had we known of her.whereabout, before she passed away.

Despite our ups and downs, I keep in touch with my family. We all care about each other, perhaps more so than those siblings who had parents to nurture their every need, especially love. To us, brought up in the harsh discipline of an orphanage, we have survived the ordeal, with little scarring.

As Mr.Lyons of the Catholic Children's Society emphasized that authorities, today, are 'struggling' to find answers why some families survive and others cannot cope.

I am still in touch with several 'old girls' from St.Anne's and it would appear most of them have had disastrous marriages, to the point were they have been physically abused by their husbands but in order to survive, decided to tolerate their 'lot'.

I have always tried to envisage my parent's plight in their marriage and do not wish to judge them too harshly for allowing my brothers, sisters and myself, to be put into institutions. It was bad eough being born in one, let alone being brought up in one. Although the pain hurts, I try not to dwell on it, as after all we have much to be thankful for in that we know who we are, and where we come from. Both sides of our family were honourable people; they were not responsible for the depression years, when families were destitute and unable to clothe and feed their children.

There are, of course, many question that can never be resolved. The mysteries surrounding the complexities of our background are known only to mother, who unfortunately has taken her secrets to the grave.

Her first husband, an Italian named Antonio Capolongo, to whom she married at the age of twenty-one in 1910, and their daughter Marie born in 1911, who passed away at sixteen months.

The mysterious Brandon, no records! How could it be possible for mother to have married this man in 1919 when she was already married to Edward Rutley Pocock Ashford in 1915, who did not divorce her until 1926. It is difficult to comprehend she was married to both men at the same time and yet, the records show this to be the case. Could this person calling herself Caroline Florence Hinks be mother, or is it perhaps Ada Florence Adams who had married Brandon and the families have been mixed up?

Over the past years I have been delving for information in the Genealogy Library at the Church of the Latter Day Saints in Victoria, who have a vast network of family records. One day I asked one of the many knowledgeable librarians why the Church was so keen on family history. Her reply was: 'if you don't know your family history and your roots, you will never know yourself.' Impressed by this piece of sound philosophy which, whilst true, it did not appear to be considered important enough or come within the scope of the Catholic Theologians to adopt this same philosophy with regard to the birthright of those children under their care. It might have been, for many of us, a different lifestyle in our adult years had we been given the choice when discharged from the orphanage, to be told our identity and family background. This, unfortunately, definitely was not the case as far as the children who were put into St.Anne's.

To come full circle, it truly is a miracle to have found our eldest brother, Charles, at seventy-two years of age, alive, having miraculously survived when his ship was torpedoed during World War II. After a lifetime of family searching, we have in our possession photographs of our parents, as well as other family members. A dream come true.

Knowing our connections to the Ashfords and Adams, my brother, sisters and I are content in the knowledge that what we have discovered about them is, without a shadow of a doubt, the truth. Although we are still puzzled with a few of the details surrounding the family history, we realize some of the mystery concerning mother will forever remain. This is something we have come to terms with, and accept. Having survived many hardships during our lives, we have been able to tell this true story of a family who through sheer willpower despite many hurdles to cross, were determined to achieve their goal in finding their roots.

About the Author

Catherine Ashford was born in London, England, one of a large family. Abandoned in infancy, she was brought up in a Catholic institution in a small village in the County of Kent. On reaching the age of sixteen she was sent out into a world she knew little of, as a domestic servant. With World War Two in progress she was conscripted into an aircraft factory in Surrey, on munition work.

When hostilities ended, she enrolled in a commercial college to train as a secretary. Emigrating to Canada in 1967, the long journey began as she sailed between England and Canada over the years, in a desperate attempt to find her missing family.

Married in 1944, she has one child.

Catherine now lives in British Columbia, Canada.

Printed in the United States
112125LV00001B/16-18/A

9 781418 478469